A Lifetime Doing Nothing

Tales, Teachings, and Testimonials

Ian McCrorie

PARIYATTI PRESS
an imprint of
Pariyatti Publishing
www.pariyatti.org

ISBN: 978-1-68172-381-5 (Print)
ISBN: 978-1-68172-384-6 (PDF)
ISBN: 978-1-68172-382-2 (ePub)
ISBN: 978-1-68172-383-9 (Mobi)
Library of Congress Control Number: 2021933870

cover photo by George and Cathie Salter

When I lost my sight…people said I was brave.
When my father left, people said I was brave.
But it is not bravery; I have no choice.
I wake up and live my life.

—Anthony Doerr

All the Light We Cannot See

Also by Ian McCrorie

The Moon Appears When the Water is Still

Children of Silence and Slow Time

For
Liam, Aiden, and Hyesun
Always

I spent a good part of my life living on a hilltop in India. This was a tribal area—many farmers, few clocks. Sunrise resonated with the sounds of cattle being taken to pasture and dusk with the sounds of the same cattle herded home for milking. In between, just a lot of silence. Perfect for what I wanted to do. And what I wanted to do was nothing.

Friends back in Canada would ask what I did all day. I faced the question head on. “Nothing,” I told them.

Incredulous, they asked, “You mean you don't do anything at all?”

“No,” I explained. “I don't do anything…”

“As we said…”

“I meant I DON’T not do not anything.”

“Can you try that again in English?”

I tried. “I do…uh…”

“What do you do?”

“I do…something,” I said.

“What?”

“Nothing.”

“We’re right back where we started!”

“Look. I do nothing. It's quite a different matter altogether from not doing anything. Capiche?”

They didn't. “Call it what you will. Either way, you're taking the easy way out. You’re a lay-about. A sloth. A slug!”

“Slugs sleep all day,” I explained. “I’m busy all day.”

“Busy? Busy doing nothing, you mean!”

“Precisely,” I said. “Besides, it isn't easy. It takes effort.”

"Yeah, I bet you work up a real sweat sitting on a cushion all day."

"Well, it's an effortless effort."

That was met with an even more incredulous look. Never one to let a metaphor simply stand or fall on its own merit, I added, "Like the sound of one hand clapping."

That did it. They threw up their hands in exasperation. They walked away unconvinced, trampling my pitiful attempt at clarification into the dust. But that was many years ago, and I thought it time to try again. I offer this little book as a more ardent, and hopefully lucid, attempt to explain the paramount importance of doing nothing.

1

I left my small hut in the tribal area of the Western Ghats of Maharashtra early one morning to go for a run through the countryside. As I came over a small rise in the road, I found myself staring at a herd of water buffalo. Each buff weighed at least 1,000 pounds and had two very sharp horns. I weighed a tenth of that and possessed no horns. As I stood mesmerized, I was quickly engulfed in a tsunami of buffs. I stood perfectly still. I had little choice to do otherwise and surprisingly fell naturally into my practice. I breathed in and out and stayed in the moment as best I could. I watched the fear demanding I flee or fight roll through my mind. Because I remained somewhat clear and calm, I understood that the former might cause a stampede and the latter was an impossibility. So, I didn't do anything. Well, that's not quite true; I did do something. I did nothing.

The buffalo walked slowly by and around me. Perhaps they realized that the 120 pounds of muscled manliness in their midst posed no threat. Or Aristaeus, the Greek god of cattle, intervened on my behalf. Regardless, the herd passed in a matter of minutes, leaving me somewhat stirred but not shaken.

I believe that most wild animals can detect our vibrations, especially fear and panic. These can spook them, and their instinct to stampede or attack takes over. Doing nothing had not only changed my life; in this particular instance and on this particular day it literally saved my life.

2

Blaise Pascal (1623–1662), a French mathematician and writer, once declared that "All of humanity's problems stem from man's inability to sit quietly in a room alone." This is the most graphic summation of the conundrum of the human condition, which is our tendency to blindly react. We scratch every itch. We are easily triggered. It seems we can't do otherwise. As Basil Fawlty said when confronted by his wife, Sybil, over his tendency to worry too much about what might happen, "But what else is there to do?" Pascal's aphorism was not so much an answer as a plea to understand the problem. Ironically, seeing the problem, understanding the extent of its reach, also opens a portal to the answer.

I, for one, seemed predisposed to convolute, to mountain every molehill, real or imagined, by blindly and/or habitually reacting to things I liked with unbridled happiness and to things I disliked with despair. I'd further compromise this conditioned reaction with other deeply ingrained co-conspirators in the guise of hope or its flip side, anxiety.

Pascal postulated that the way to transcend all my self-induced histrionics was to cultivate the skill "to sit quietly in a room alone." In essence, to do nothing, letting our conditioned and habitual responses just lie there, simmering away, without jumping in and stirring up an already boiling pot of conundrum. Two thousand years before Pascal, Lao Tzu called this skill *wéiwúwéi*, or "doing non-doing."

3

Self-introspection is not the strongest attribute of *Homo sapiens*. Our forefathers survived primarily because they were men of action, fleeing or fighting as the situation demanded. And they hunted in groups, perhaps the only time they were quiet. Sound familiar? Of course it does, because we as a species haven't evolved much, especially as far as the mind is concerned. Many men brag today of their sixty, eighty, even one-hundred-hour workweeks, promoting a kind of toil glamor. Women seem to want it all: career, full-time mother, charity volunteer, marathoner. As well, Pascal's observation might prove problematic today for the simple reason that it is impossible to spare enough time to find an empty room, let alone an interval to simply sit there by yourself. And forget about the quietly part—there are e-mails and tweets requiring immediate attention.

The first time I attempted to sit quietly in a room alone, my body soon began to fidget. I couldn't seem to get comfortable. I blamed, in order, the cushion underneath me, the temperature in the room, and the sunlight streaming in the window. My mind ran amok, flitting first here and then there like some wild monkey, devoid of rhyme or reason. Any attempt at discursive thought or analysis or even the simple observation of my breath was shunted aside by flashbacks, memories, plans, hopes, fears. Very soon, a craving for distraction arose. I was desperate for a book to read, some music to listen to, a movie to watch, or a bag of Doritos to chow down on.

My self-image was quite shaken. I was shocked to realize my mind resembled an Energizer Bunny on steroids. It appeared to run on a loop of hyperactive blind reactions to whatever popped up into my consciousness. I thought I was crazy. I talked to my teacher. "Yes, yes, you are crazy," he told me. "But now at least you know it. Only sane people realize just how crazy they are."

I realized I was Basil Fawlty at heart! I had been raging and winging over every trifling insult or comeuppance in my life until exasperation and apoplectic reactivity were my fallback positions. I lived in a constant state of panic because what else is there to do?! What else, indeed.

4

Because I had seldom, if ever, sat quietly in a room alone, the irony was that I thought my mind was akin to a well-oiled Bianchi racing bike. Of course, I was totally deluded. I had equated intelligence, literacy, strong opinions, and popularity with a beautiful mind—a Bianchi, if you will. In fact, my mind more resembled that rusted old clunker in the back of the garage. Two Israeli psychologists, Daniel Tversky and Amos Kahneman, experts in rusted old clunkers, spoke to this seeming contradiction. They concluded that "We think that we are much more rational than we are. We think we make our decisions because we have good reasons to make them... [Yet] it's the other way around. We believe in the reasons because we've already made the decision." So like a deluded statistician, I had drawn a straight line from an unwarranted assumption to a foregone conclusion.

Many decades later, the good news is that I can assure you that a well-oiled Bianchi racing bike does lie somewhere within all of us, but it resides buried under the detritus of hyperactive and delusional thinking patterns. These rust and prematurely age your Bianchi. But there is even better news and it is threefold.

First, Blaise Pascal was spot on. In my experience, all our problems do indeed stem from this hyperactive and delusional thinking we have acquired over time.

Second, there is a way to eradicate the light-speed, blind reactions and the habitual confusion.

And third, the way is very simple. It boils down to just two words: do nothing. That's it. Do nothing. Sit quietly in a room alone and do nothing. Watch the monkey mind and do not try to fix it or eliminate it or drown it out or engage it.

This is doing non-doing. Observe the mind, on autopilot as usual, screaming editorial comments from the sidelines like some frenzied play-by-play announcer and *do* nothing about it. Don't turn the monologue into a dialogue. Do nothing. "Nothing to see here, folks. Let's keep it moving."

Unlike Basil Fawlty, you calmly abide the diatribe. "But what else is there to do?" Only one thing. You do non-doing. And over time, the mind calms. And as the panic subsides, the mind gains insight into its own machinations. This insight removes some, most or all of the detritus covering the well-oiled Bianchi. Doing non-doing helps you find what you never lost.

What is interesting for me is that almost everyone catches fleeting glimpses of this non-doing mind from time to time. They may not understand what it was at the time, only that it was an unexplainable, peaceful interlude that came out of the blue. I had two such interludes which I didn't understand until much later in my life but for which I am thankful nevertheless, for they planted seeds of possibility in my deeper subconscious.

5

My first revelation occurred on a Friday evening just before my first year of university. I had the book list I needed for my courses, and a friend drove me to the uni bookstore. Books in hand, I felt quite chuffed. I had used my own money. I felt independent and responsible. On the drive home, my friend suggested we go out to a party. I declined. I don't know why. Perhaps it just felt like, if not the right thing to do, at least the only comfortable choice I could make.

That evening I sat at home with my mother, my pile of books beside me on the couch. I skimmed each and every book, devoured their smell, and savored the anticipated lectures that would unlock the secrets they contained. I was happy, ecstatically so. I could have stayed on that couch forever.

However, the introverted, solitary dweeb that showed up that Friday night was soon overwhelmed with cravings for alcohol and parties and popularity. It was the times, the swingin' sixties. Hard to resist at eighteen. So I dug myself into a hole and for the next ten years continued to dig deeper. What else was there to do?! But that singular evening of quiet certitude would arise in my mind from time to time, letting me know that living in an alcoholic and drug-induced fog might not have to be my fallback position.

6

My second epiphany took place after university, when I was teaching grade eight. I was on the front line, trying to hold the raging hormones of thirty-six students at bay long enough to stuff some important knowledge into their overly coiffed little heads. I found it necessary to take a few mental health days, usually in the spring. For this respite from the tedium of incarceration in a sweat-sock-stench of a classroom I made no plans, mentally inscribed no schedule, nor looked forward to any particular aspect of the gifted day.

I awoke full of energy, breakfasted, and walked out the door, eager to find where my feet would take me. Though I was familiar enough with my general environs, I was unaware of where I was going; I was aware only that I was going. It was the middle of a workweek. I was playing truant, which is, in and of itself, an intoxicant. I felt as if my life sentence for some hideous crime had been reprieved by an insightful and beneficent judge. A free day to myself, immersed with possibilities, including the freedom to actualize absolutely none of them. I held no obligations to anyone, not even to said judge. Because it was a free day, I could waste time on a second cup of coffee in a café. I could scroll through a magazine I never usually even glanced at. I could circumvent some of my presumptions about who I was. The day was less at my disposal than I was at the disposal of the day. I was just along for the ride.

Only years later did I realize I had been doing non-doing that day, actively engaging the unconditioned mind to direct my steps. I had found, if only for a few hours, what I had never lost. I was aware of everything I did, while ignoring all the shoulds and musts and coulds, all the conditioning elements.

Soon enough, of course, I returned to the status quo, behaving as I always had, thinking like my peers and parents. Ah, but for that one unscripted day I caught a glimpse of freedom. While it is true that one swallow does not a summer make, my two swallows acted as harbingers for an eventual endless summer.

7

If it is not already clear, it cannot be emphasized often enough that non-doing is not lethargy. Nor is it apathy, sloth, or laziness. It is not complacency or inactivity. It is not relaxation or spacing out. It is, however, a conscious effort to calmly abide the push-me, pull-me, come-hither beckoning of old habit patterns. At a deeper level, before we do anything, before we fight or take flight, before we speak harshly or critically, before we even lift a finger, neurotransmitters in different parts of our mind have been hard at work judging, comparing, remembering, hoping, and fearing, and then mixing all these disparate elements into a primordial soup, spicing the whole mess with our predispositions, idiosyncrasies, and habitual tendencies. Just as rainwater follows the well-worn gullies and troughs down the hill, our reactions to different situations are preordained. "We've already made the decision." Non-doing simply and calmly observes the mind's siren call to action.

Doing nothing is an introspective skill for understanding what is going on in the mind. This skill is active in that it requires effort, but it is an effortless effort, much "like a man with no hands making a fist" according to Roshi Albert Low. Perspiration is not involved. Alertness is. Being present. Mindful. Without these things, old habit patterns, relentless in their subterfuge to get us to behave as we always have, or you might say as we have been trained to do, would continue to rule the roost. They have been so successful in this regard that we may think these patterns express our true nature. Far from it, as we shall see. Calmly abiding the machinations of the mind holds their narcotic control over us at bay.

8

So that's it. It is really that simple. Sit alone in a room quietly. Keeping the spine as straight as possible will help to keep lethargy at bay. At first it is normal to feel somewhat self-conscious, so be aware of any tendency to offset your apprehension by going overboard, attempting to mimic a pencil-thin *sādhu* from Benares. This is not a photo op for the cover of "Serenity Now!" What you are doing, or better, not doing is not very special. It is no big deal. Sitting is just providing the mind with lots of space. Meditation should be seen as normal as apple pie because, as Ajahn Chah pointed out, "Even ducks sit."

So sit. And do so quietly, which should be easy, for the simple reason that you are alone. There is no temptation to engage anyone in conversation. Or so I thought, until I quickly realized it wasn't others I needed to be concerned about. It was me who was not quiet. Not only that, I was actually engaged in conversation. I was in fact jabbering away a mile a minute. Mind you, the dialogue was between me and myself. I was quite surprised at how unquiet I was. With hindsight, this was very good to see this. In fact, it was really the lesson of the day. The lesson actually of many days! Something can't be righted until the depth of the conundrum is understood.

For the first time, I had caught a glimpse of the monkey mind and saw how crazy it was. I saw how this wonderful mind of mine, the one that got me into university, seemed to be on autopilot commenting on everything I did or thought, judging, lamenting, praising, digging deeper and deeper pathways that facilitated the flow of dopamine (believe it or not, the mind feels good feeling bad), so I wanted to travel those pathways over and over again. And so, I did. And still, to an extent, do.

But when doing non-doing, this is perfectly fine, because the internal chatter is not trying to be eradicated. I'm not trying to find my happy place. I'm not trying to sit in the silence of now. I'm not trying to do anything. I'm not trying…period. I am observing the present state of my mind and body and doing nothing about it.

The task is to remain awake to all the chatter. Just watch it, see it as it arises, stays a while and naturally and inevitably quiets, and then passes away when it is in all likelihood replaced by another round of chattering. Awareness, though, is now in the driver's seat. And beside awareness sits equanimity, an internal calmness, a half-smile at the seeming futility of the task at hand. Like two wings of a bird, they maintain balance. The tandem of awareness and equanimity provides the remedy to all our woes. (Why be unhappy about something if it can be remedied? And what is the use of being unhappy about something if it cannot be remedied?) Yogic breath awareness and mantras and concentration practices have been around since the beginning of history. But it was the Buddha who emphasized awareness and equanimity, the tag team "doing" component of non-doing.

~ 9

Two and a half thousand years ago, the Buddha summed up his discovery, "mind matters most." *Buddha*, meaning "the awakened one," is an honorific for Siddhartha Gautama, a Śākyan prince from northern India. He practiced what is called in Pāli *ātāpīsampajānosatimā*, "ardently, mindfully, thoughtfully" maintaining awareness with a clear understanding of what is going on in the mind at every moment. In other words, doing non-doing while remaining awake to the whole firestorm. Engaged non-engagement. There is nothing holy or even spiritual about the work. Insight into the mind's goings on is more a scientific investigation.

The whole deal, the big kahuna of the human enigma, the Buddha referred to as "conditioning." We are conditioned by our family, our friends, our religion, and society in general, influencing who we think we are and what we think we wish to become. Conditioning taints our view of reality and our goals and dreams. Rabindranath Tagore, the great Indian poet, observed that "We read the world wrong and say that it deceives us." Conditioning is akin to holding a map upside down, getting completely lost, and doing it over again and again because everyone else is using the very same map, and most are also holding it incorrectly.

As we see into this conditioned mind, how we have been deceived, the way it coerces us to react to our emotions, our memories, our hopes, and our fears, we uncover the forces at play in creating "me." Calmly abiding the conditioning process loosens the grip these forces have on our attention. As the chatter in the mind calms, we get a glimpse of the unconditioned mind, the state of pure awareness. For a brief moment, we are free of any desire to attain or become something special. We begin to see things not as we are conditioned to see them but as they really are.

And how are things really? The Buddha discovered four noble truths, or laws. Just as Newton's revelation of gravity allowed others to better understand everything from falling apples to the orbits of distant planets, the Buddha outlined these four laws as a scientist would, asking if anyone could prove his laws wrong. Almost three millennia later, he is still waiting for someone to speak up.

Ajahn Amaro explains the four laws as a doctor might. First, the Buddha analyzes and explains the symptoms of the discomfort. The second law reveals the root cause of the distress. Third, the Buddha gives the prognosis. (It is good, by the way.) And finally, based on his own experiment (on himself) he outlines the methodology or prescription to rid you of whatever is ailing you.

10

The yin-yang symbol is a graphic illustration of the human condition. What is pictured at the left represents your symptoms, which is to say, the first noble truth. Light represents happiness, gain, good health, etc., and darkness represents unhappiness, loss, poor health, etc. Light and dark dance in a fluid relationship. Another metaphor for light and dark is order and chaos. Some call it good and evil, conjuring biblical imagery. Regardless of the nomenclature, yin and yang are dynamic natural forces. At different times, yin encroaches into yang and yang encroaches into yin, with neither able to overwhelm the other thanks to the counterweights of the opposite force found in each. When darkness floods the mind, there remains a circle of light that prevents drowning. And when light permeates the mind, an undercurrent of sadness resonates that this won't last forever. This helps subdue any mania.

This is the unconditioned mind in its natural state. This is the non-doing mind. This is the beginner's mind that Suzuki-roshi encouraged us to watch with child-like wonder. This is the natural mind. Moods come and go, emotions roller-coaster up and down, ideas and ruminations light up the night sky only to fall back to earth with dawn's sobering second thought. Simply watch it all arise and fall without getting involved in the soap opera. Nothing is broken in the interplay between yin and yang. When life goes awry, suffering grows only when we attempt to play Mr. Fix-it. Such is the cause of our *dukkha*, as the Buddha called suffering. *Dukkha* sums up the human condition. Its existence, as a law of nature, is the first noble truth.

11

If *dukkha*, "suffering" or "unsatisfactoriness," is the first noble truth, wherein lies its cause? The Buddha discovered that the root of suffering lies in the human tendency to involve ourselves in the yin-yang roller-coaster, to try to fix what we perceive to be broken. We naturally want to prolong the pleasant and rid ourselves of the unpleasant. We are attracted to things we think will make us happy, and we are repulsed by the things that depress us. We crave what we feel is pleasant, and we abhor what we feel is unpleasant. We like the yin and hate the yang. However, these are naturally occurring forces like rain and sun. Wanting to perpetually bask in the sun and completely eradicate the rain is simply delusional.

And sadly, we are deluded, ignorant of how the mind works. We are like helicopter parents with children in the neighborhood sandbox, refusing to simply let the children play. They want to control the process and maximize the fun, without anyone getting their clothes dirty. This greed and aversion and general ignorance compound the darkness, lengthening its stay and holding the imminent arrival of light at bay. This dissatisfaction exacerbates the craving and abhorrence in an already conditioned mind. Greed is like trying to assuage your thirst by drinking saltwater—the more you drink the thirstier you become. It is like scratching an itch on your foot with a boot on.

This then is the second noble truth.

12

A man walked into his doctor's office and told him he was not doing well. He was in pain all over. "Everywhere I touch, it hurts," he said. The good doctor gave him a battery of tests, all of which came up negative. Then the doctor had a brain wave.

"Broken finger," proclaimed the doctor.

This comedic metaphor evokes what we are dealing with. Everything is unsatisfactory, pain seems to last forever, and initial joy eventually wanes. "Everywhere I touch, it hurts." This is of course delusional. The hurt is not out there, in everything. It is what I touch everything with that is "broken." This finger of the old vaudeville joke is the conditioned mind. Ajahn Sumedho is very clear about this. "It's not the self that is the problem; it's our delusions around the *perceptions* of what we are, the conditioning of the mind we acquire after birth... through our parents, our peers, and the society we live in." We need to access the mind in its unconditioned state from before we were born. But first we must wake up to the conditioned mind and uncover its pernicious nature if we want to be free. Every time we blindly react, as we have been conditioned to do, we reinforce that very conditioning. We become what we repeatedly do. Ajahn Sumedho warns us that "If you think you have a problem with fear, you will keep recreating fear." It is no wonder it hurts everywhere.

To return to the medical metaphor for a minute, the fact that everything is unsatisfactory, *dukkha*, is the symptom of our illness. This symptom is so pervasive, so omnipresent, and our mind is so conditioned by greed, hatred, and delusion that our inner Basil Fawlty takes over and demands "What can we do about it?" Keats answered him hundreds of years before: "Now more than ever seems it rich to die, To cease upon the midnight with no pain." It is sad to imagine that even as great a writer as Keats saw death as the only way out of the *dukkha* of his conditioned mind.

The Buddha, ever the scientist, was convinced that there had to be a better way; a route to overcome or transcend the cause of suffering had to be possible. This was his hypothesis. He reasoned that if he could uncover the cause of this dissatisfaction and eliminate it, then *dukkha* would end. His hypothesis was the third noble truth.

It could only earn the label of truth when and if he indeed transcended suffering. More than that, to earn the label of a natural law, a scientific proof, it must be possible to replicate the method that would accomplish transcendence. He looked within for eight years until he saw in a flash one night that suffering arises when we crave the order of life or abhor the chaos or simply don't understand that the whole show is subject to change. Yin morphs into yang and vice versa over time. Adding craving to one and abhorrence to the other, all the while deluded by "What else is there to do?" is the broken finger. And the Buddha saw what was broken and healed it.

This journey of discovery, with many false leads and abandoned theories, eventually coalesced into the fourth noble truth. The Buddha called it a path composed of eight components covering all aspects of doing non-doing, from morality to concentration and understanding. Life may be painful a lot of the time and not very satisfactory at the best of those times, but the path of doing non-doing alleviates much, if not all, of the ensuing suffering.

13

Norwegian author Karl Ove Knausgaard wrote in *My Struggle* of a time when he was very sick. He couldn't move, and he lay on the sofa the whole day feeling miserable. His inability to move meant he was lying quietly in a room alone (Pascal would have approved). It proved impossible for him to escape his pain by engaging in some physical activity. More to the point, he surrendered to his misery. He remained present to every excruciating moment. Yet he didn't lapse into sorrow or depression. He wrote that he "enjoyed every second" of his ordeal. His to-do list for the day lay in tatters on the floor, e-mails remained unopened, and phone calls went directly to voice mail. The pain remained, but the ensuing suffering abated, proof positive of the underlying spot of light in the sea of darkness in the unconditioned mind. Pain is inevitable in life, suffering, an option. There may be many extraneous reasons for our pain, but the ensuing and continuing suffering, the self-victimizing, is wholly our own responsibility.

Viktor Frankl was a holocaust survivor who survived the death camps of the Nazis by keeping love in his heart. He later wrote eloquently of our need to live a life free of victimization, because "the one thing you can't take away from me is the way I choose to respond to what you do to me."

From those who feel hard-done by forces outside their control, you often hear the admonishment "Don't rain on my parade." At a literal level rain is simply water droplets devoid of any intention, malicious or otherwise. It too is a condition, and like those of the mind, it passes. Furthermore, that was no parade you had going there before it started raining. People walking behind you in the same direction do not constitute a parade, even if they are carrying trombones.

My teacher, facing the inevitable question from a neophyte about how long his knee pain might last or some variation of that would reply that he had no idea. Maybe it will last the rest of your life. Maybe it will never go away. So accept it, let it be, and get on with your life and the tasks at hand.

14

Many of us are busy with the business of being busy, and Knausgaard was no exception. His writing explores the busyness of his mind, especially with how he deals with his family. He explores the conditioned mind with objective honesty. Being busy can often be an affirmation of our status as an important cog in the world. Without our constant input and energy, everything will fall apart, won't it? Busyness masks all our doubts and fears concerning our self-worth. They disappear beneath a veneer of smiling competence and go-for-it energy. This failure to really see what lurks in the deep recesses of our mind leads to many bouts of existential angst, staring at harsh reality, worrying that we are not whom we appear to be. And of course, we aren't. None of us is. We are all subjected to ongoing conditioning by the pressures surrounding us, our personas crafted and fine-tuned, adding another coating of veneer onto who I think I am.

You may recall the admonition of Henry David Thoreau in *Walden*: "Simplicity, simplicity, simplicity! I say, let your affairs be as two or three, and not a hundred or a thousand; instead of a million count half a dozen, and keep your accounts on your thumbnail." Busyness, both in our environment and in our mind, rings the death knell for peace, love, and understanding.

Busyness is an unskillful response to an agitated mind with its excess worries and feelings of guilt. By immersing ourselves in our work, our family, our avocations, or our addictions we hope to hold our negative mental anxieties at bay. This may work in the short term, but we will eventually crash from exhaustion. We need rest. We need quiet, even solitude. But then again, we fear that quiet solitude itself is the playground for all the negative conditions of the mind that we hope we have been suppressing. Any easing up on the accelerator of busyness might allow all the fearful negativities and guilt and worries to bubble up onto the surface of the mind. Faced by now-strengthened anxieties, we double down on our busyness, forming a negative feedback loop that knows no end, a Möbius strip of misery.

Simplicity is not a plea for poverty but a way to lessen the complications and unexpected consequences arising from excess in our personal lives, in society, and in our own mind. We fall prey to the temptations of more when our mind is in turmoil with the hope that more or better or different will assuage the caterwauling. True wealth does not require more riches than anyone else but contentment with what we have. And contentment can only arise in silence.

15

The Pirahã natives live in the upper Amazon rain forest. Daniel Everett is one of only three linguists who can speak their language. He lived with them for many years and discovered through their language that they appear to be the only people on Earth who live in the here and now. They are fully present to their life in each moment.

They do not have a number system. Without a sense of how much one has compared to another, there is little jealousy. They don't strive to accumulate more. When they are hungry, they hunt. They have no word for yesterday or tomorrow. When someone has paddled by canoe out of their sight, they do not ask when he will return or how long he will be gone. He has gone from their mind. They have no permanent dwellings. Children are loved and nourished.

Everett arrived in their community as a Christian missionary. Conversion proved impossible because they could not understand talking about someone who wasn't in front of them at that moment. They had no words for that concept. Over time conversion was accomplished, but it was not the Pirahã who took to the Bible. Everett was the one converted. He chose the happiness of this moment, simply being present. He became the richest man in the world when he was with the Pirahã, because he didn't need more. Even this little in front of him now was enough. The Norwegians have a word for this: *lagom*, "even this is enough."

This is not a Timothy Leary argument to drop out, quit your job, and live on nuts and berries. It is an argument for a life of clarity in which we remain awake, aware, and calm, seeing things as they really are and understanding the role that habituated greed, abhorrence, and delusion play on our mind.

We begin to understand the difference between wants and needs. This is a noble pursuit, no more or less for a penniless mendicant than an accountant in Topeka.

16

Watch a baby for a while and you can't help but see how hard they are working. They are looking out on the world, trying to make sense of it all. They focus on this and then they focus on that. They react, sometimes with tears, ofttimes with a smile, indications that they have assessed the situation and found it wanting or fulfilling. When you place them on the floor, they try to raise their head, the better to see something besides carpeting. Once this is mastered, they move on to face new challenges. First standing, then walking, falling down with both endeavors. And so on it goes. The work of life never stops. In fact, even Nietzsche and Darwin agree on this one thing, namely that life is striving. Whether you get paid for your efforts or not is another matter, but you will strive. Horace thought that "life grants nothing to us mortals without hard work."

Modern lives are built around our work. If we love what we do, we may not even think of it as work. Bobby Orr, the great Boston Bruin hockey player, was once asked, given his wonky knees, whether he was thinking of retiring. He answered in the negative, adding, "I'm too young to get a real job." Along the same lines a good friend of mine was threatened with downsizing due to government cutbacks. To buck him up I suggested that this may open an opportunity to do what he really wanted to do. He replied that he was already doing what he really wanted to do.

But for most of us, work is merely tolerable, at least for a while. We delay our gratification in return for the salary which provides us a place to live and a means of transportation, and if we earn enough, sufficient resources to indulge in a few outside interests. It is a contract. Since you've signed on, you might as well give it your all, work honestly, and contribute positively to the workspace. If you can't do this, then you should seek another line of work before resentment sets in, tilting your mind towards nefarious rewards to console your misery.

Whether you are president of the world or washing dishes in a diner, do it well, giving it all your full attention. It is your duty, your role, and your contribution to do what is at hand this moment. You dishonor yourself, those you are serving, and the job itself when you turn away from the simple task at hand to indulge in illusions of retribution and delusions of escape. Habituated internal chatter, wishing to be somewhere else, doing something else, with somebody else prevents natural joy and wonder from arising. And our occupation, more than any other endeavor provides us a daily opportunity to simply do what we are doing. Keep it simple, one task at a time garnering all your attention.

An integral part of all Zen retreats is the work period. The work is assigned without regard for hierarchy or seniority. It could involve sweeping the grounds, doing the dishes, preparing tea, or cleaning the latrine. The actual work is secondary to bringing the sitting practice into an activity closer to real life, especially the jobs that you try to rush through or even avoid. Many of us, faced with those tasks, put on headphones and escape into the music, but on Zen retreats there are no exits. You are asked to pay attention every waking minute.

17

This story is from Toni Packer, the late, much-venerated Zen teacher. A student asks a Zen master for some principles of the highest wisdom.

The master replies, "Attention."

"Is that it?" asks the student. "Nothing to add?"

The teacher says, "Attention. Attention!"

The student is getting frustrated. He feels misunderstood or even somewhat slighted. The master, being a true master, feels his frustration and so repeats, "Attention. Attention. Attention!"

The student surrenders but still feels he is missing something. In desperation he finally asks, "What does attention mean anyway?"

The teacher smiles and replies, "Attention means attention."

Attention is doing non-doing. Attention is not the word "attention." In the same vein, doing non-doing is not the words "doing non-doing." Can there be attention, can there be doing non-doing without your being present, "paying" attention, without your "doing" the doing non-doing?

Another Zen story speaking to this point concerns some students sitting with their teacher near a flagpole. The wind was blowing and the flag was flapping. One of the students asked, "Why is the flag flapping? It must be because of the wind."

Another spoke up and said, "No. It's because there is a flag." The debate raged on. "…because of the wind…" "…because of the flag." On and on until finally the teacher spoke.

"You're both wrong. And that is the reason the flag is flapping and flapping. There is no flag, and there is no wind."

No flag. No wind. No me. No you. No separation. And when you see that, the flapping of the flag and the flapping of the mind are no longer problems.

18

Be here now. Just three words. Be here now. The oft-heard teaching is eminently simple but absolutely profound. Happiness can only be found in this moment, in the here and now. Living in the past will inevitably lead to regrets, guilt, fears, and enough "should haves" to fill a black hole. Living in the idyllic valleys of tomorrow land leads to idle speculation, hopes and dreams that quickly spin us into anxiety and neuroses based on a bottomless pit of "what ifs."

Anxiety disorders affect 18.1% of the American adult (ages 18–54) population, a number bound to go up when recent findings of the adverse psychological effects on younger teens due to excessive smart phone use are factored in. Dread, the unnatural fear of what might be, haunts all those who flee the simple joy of living in this moment, watching it unfold without undue comment.

Thich Nhat Hanh has written a lovely little book called *How to Walk*. He speaks of walking as a meditation practice. He urges us to just walk and be aware of the process of walking. Lifting the foot, placing it down, lifting the back foot, bending the knee, etc. As we just walk, we become aware, maybe for the first time in our life, of the smells around us, the feeling of the sun on the back of our neck, the simple joy of being alive. Stay in this moment. Over time, with practice, being in this moment either as we walk, talk, or drive a car becomes second nature to us. We dwell less and less in the past and the future and experience a profound joy in this very moment, free of the need to analyze it, philosophize about it, sanctify it. We are the walking. It is perfect as it is. You just need to stay out of it, it needn't concern you. As a matter of fact, it's none of your damn business.

19

I am waiting for Thich Nhat Hanh to write a follow-up book, *How to Listen*, to address the proliferation of PMPs (personal music players). Many young people walk everywhere, ear-budded to all the music ever created, oblivious to the sounds around and within them. They drown out the inner chaos, making it all the stronger and more frightening when they are not buddedup. And they tune out the natural music of the city, the symphony of cacophony and crisis and traffic flow and horns honking and even, sometimes, birdsong.

Hear the sounds around you, being aware of subtle and not-so-subtle reactions to them. This is hearing non-hearing, leaving the sounds at your ear and remaining calm (but aware) of dislikes and enjoyments as one sound pushes out another. When I practice in this way, I call it "wearing my air-buds."

For a while I lived in a Buddhist forest monastery in West Virginia. This was a staunchly Evangelical Christian area of the state. Our neighbors to the west of us did not take too kindly to us with our ochre robes and shaved heads. They would sneak into our dorm when we were asleep and slip Christian pamphlets under our sleeping bags. It was summer, and the heat coerced us to meditate outside on some flat rocks in full view of our neighbors. This set them off to no end, and they retaliated by buying their teenage son the drum set he always wanted. He as well took to practicing outside. Every time we convened outside to meditate seemed to coincide with his practice time. I mentioned how agitating I found this incursion into my solitude to my senior, Bhante Rahula, who asked me if the noise was bothering me or was it me bothering the noise?

Doing nothing about our reactions, calmly abiding our tendencies to grab onto every perceived injustice, becoming in the process prosecutor, judge, and jury, all in one, alters everything. I began to see the drumming as sensations at my ear sense-door, and I developed some compassion for the teen boy who was made to drum simply to cause us distress, a singularly uncharitable action for a Christian. And think of the poor mother, so fearful of two strangely attired young men sitting outside with their eyes closed. She certainly needed lots of compassion and understanding.

20

A few years after living as a monk in West Virginia, I stayed a while at Wat Pah Nanachat near the Mekong River in Ubon in Thailand. This was the real deal. A forest monastery with *dhuthaṅga* monks who adopted thirteen additional vows, including taking only one meal a day and practicing other severities. We would rise about 4:00 am, meditate, and then go on *pindipat*, a 2,500-year-old tradition of collecting alms from the local villages. Please note this was not begging, as the monks asked for nothing. They even refrained from making eye contact with the laity that lined up on the roadside. Consequently, the act of giving food remains as pure and uncoerced as possible. After returning to the monastery, while the collected food was reheated, the monks attended to house cleaning chores, filling the urns with water, and sweeping the walking paths. After all that, the one meal of the day was consumed.

What surprised me the most was that the day was quite full with mundane chores. I had presumed it was full-on meditation 24/7. However, I found the monks to a one to be exactly as I had expected: peaceful, kind, loving, and very focused. With such little time devoted to formal practice, how could that be? As I observed them going about their business, I got my answer. They did everything with awareness and equanimity. Nothing was hurried. They spent a lot of time each day adjusting their robes. They waited for fellow monks, for the arrival of the abbot, for the food bowls to be passed to them with patience, grace and gratitude. This moment-to-moment doing non-doing was their practice.

For the past two years, my wife has returned to school. She is training to be a nurse, and the hours are brutal. When she is home, she is in the den studying…or asleep. My formal practice has gone out the window, but thanks to my time in Thailand and Burma I maintain a daily practice focusing on the often overlooked, more often disdained small jobs that hold a household together. I go food shopping and take a primordial satisfaction that we always have food aplenty. I make beds, do a wash, hang out clothes to dry, iron my wife's uniforms, make lunches, and generally pick up detritus that my sons have dropped. The latter is a full-time job in itself, perhaps my domestic equivalent of the monks adjusting the folds of their robes.

My moment-to-moment awareness is helped greatly by pausing. After I stand up, I pause, even for just a nanosecond before I walk into the kitchen. I pause at the refrigerator before I place my hand on the handle. And I pause again before I pull on the handle, opening the refrigerator door. The pause re-establishes awareness that often gets sidetracked with activity. Over time when awareness is more established, the pause may not be discernable to anyone watching you. And of course, eventually awareness may be so strongly present that all activity is simply one prolonged pause.

So, I am living a small life these days. Small perhaps, even trivial by nature, but surprisingly full of challenges and countless opportunities to perform every task with awareness and equanimity. I am very grateful for this opportunity to be a monastic *hausfrau*. My wife paid me the ultimate compliment by telling me that one day I would make somebody a good wife. I'd agree as long as she was my husband.

21

Marcus Aurelius, the great Stoic philosopher, makes it clear how important it is to be present: "The longest and shortest lives amount to the same, for the present moment is equal to everyone." Just one mindful moment is all you need to stand firm against the habitual temptations to engage, to follow, to blindly react to greed, hatred, and delusion. That one mindful moment, pregnant with peaceful profundity, will become two and two, three until inevitably, miracle of miracles, you simply walk the walk.

I once lived in a yoga ashram in rural Pennsylvania. To earn our keep we all did service around the ashram, and my service, or *seva*, as we called it, was washing dishes. We had a full professional kitchen and served over 200 meals a day, as we had many guests who came to learn yoga. There were many dishes and lots of pots and pans the size of silos. When I finished the breakfast dishes, in would come the kitchenware from the lunch prep, followed by the lunch dishes, followed by the dinner prep, followed by…it was endless. I tried the first week to get the job done on time. I worked very fast and collapsed from exhaustion. I had given my all.

As I recovered, I realized the problem. I had assumed my job was to finish the dishes. My job was to wash all the dishes. It wasn't. I couldn't do that, no one could. There were simply too many. But I could wash one dish. And that was what I started to do. One dish at a time, washing only the one that was in my hand at that moment. Lamenting my workload depleted my energy but washing one dish at a time I could handle that. And I washed that one item all day long for many weeks. I never finished the dishes. The work was never done. However, it became a joyful experience. I washed the dishes to wash the dishes.

Ajahn Pasanno tells a similar tale. When talking to his fellow monks, especially those on the leaf-sweeping detail, about the work period one day, he encouraged them by noting that there really wasn't so much to do. Now this would come as a surprise to anyone who has ever spent anytime in a Thai jungle, but he went on to explain, "just sweep what is in front of your broom."

Live the life in front of you. This too is a Stoic prescription for happiness best expressed millennia later by Walt Whitman in "Leaves of Grass."

> That you are here—that life exists and identity,
> That the powerful play goes on, and you may contribute a verse.

22

To repeat, all man's problems stem from an inability to sit alone in a room in silence. However, Pascal omitted to say that sitting alone in silence in such a room is not easy. It can be so difficult, in fact, that it unbalances the mind. It can be so frustrating that scientists tested how far people would go to avoid difficulties that ran the spectrum from boredom to hyperactivity. In the test, student volunteers surrendered all their devices and sat alone in a darkened room. They were told that if it got too much for them, they could push a small button to receive an electric shock. Alone with just their thoughts, almost 25% of the volunteers shocked themselves to take their mind off their…mind! This seems to indicate that even if someone is totally on board with the why and how of meditation, ignorant habitual responses to doing non-doing are bound to arise from time to time. And in my experience, the quieter the mind becomes, the louder seem the voices of despair.

Our misery, dissatisfaction, unhappiness, and agitation, however, should not be perceived as a problem. We hate problems. Problems need to be fixed. Anything that is problematic needs to be solved as soon as possible. It is what we do best. In America, problem-solvers, from psychiatrists to lawyers to lifestyle coaches and personal trainers, yoga teachers, and self-help gurus, cover the landscape.

Misery, however, does not require eradication. It is a condition of the mind. It often arises for perfectly understandable reasons. It's patently obvious that life, from time to time, can be very painful. It is only reasonable as well to want to eradicate my pain, take a pill, and watch television. The reactions themselves are also natural conditions of the mind. Pay attention, stay alert. Do nothing. Remain awake to the natural ebb and flow of despair and exaltation. Do nothing but stay awake.

What is really at the heart of doing non-doing is making the unconscious mind conscious. Deep-rooted aspects of our psyche that have troubled us for years, though we may not have been aware of their impact, may begin to bubble up to the surface. They may arrive as unfinished business. Call them what you will. Truth is, now these festering quagmires have come for their due. Facing them calmly and quietly and clearly comprehending what is going on requires strong determination, because what is asked for is to do nothing. Eradication is neither possible nor healthy. Stuff has happened. Things have been done. These are facts, and they can't be undone. However, bravely accepting events and facing the suffering head-on will lessen their subterfuge.

Another thing to be clear about is that you can't do it. It can be done, but *you*, the great problem-solver, *you*, the center of the universe, have to get out of the way. If *you* get involved *you* will crave to solve the problem, and *you* will hate the problem when it sticks around, because *you* remain deluded that all your old approaches to problems should still work. But ask yourself why would the very thought processes, the great problem-solving app hard-wired into your mind, that got you into the mess in the first place, be able to clean up that same mess? It is akin to pasting feathers on a volleyball hoping for a duck.

You can't do it, but it can be done. Meditation is going on, doing non-doing is being done, but there is no one meditating, no one understanding, no one getting happier. Doing non-doing is a form of internal housecleaning, but one in which the carpeting is removed so that the habit of sweeping the dust of conditioning under it is no longer a viable alternative. This deconditioning results in a cleaner, clearer, and less judgmental and habitual mind.

23

"We are going to die, and that makes us the lucky ones. Most people are never going to die because they are never going to be born. The potential people who could have been here in my place but who will in fact never see the light of day outnumber the sand grains of Arabia." So wrote Richard Dawkins in *Unweaving the Rainbow*.

We are lucky to be alive. We should be grateful. As the mind deconditions, as the simple joys of small things begin to pervade our being, we fill with gratitude just to be alive here now, to see and feel all this, holding the whole universe, as William Blake said, in a grain of sand.

A sense of gratitude struggles to arise because its sublime simplicity is overwhelmed by the cacophony of raucous voices imploring our attention. Non-doing calms the tumult, allowing gratitude for the perfection of every moment to quietly assume its rightful place in the forefront of our mind. Gratitude softens the jagged edges of past trauma and welcomes the investigative Q-Tip probe of awareness to get into all the nooks and crannies, dislodging the impacted ear wax of negative mind states. The unconscious underpinnings become conscious. Eventually we let go, we let it all just be. Doing nothing but leaving nothing undone.

24

As a child, I did not seek out thrills or danger of any kind. I did not enjoy games or contests or practical jokes. I hated costume parties. I'd rather go for a walk with my friends or sit and talk and have tea. Even today, I really don't need fun. And these post-salaried days, I don't do much of anything. I am not purpose driven. I find stimulation in the simplest of things. Carry water and hew wood, so to speak. I am frugal because I can't find much of value on which to spend money.

I am quite happy, despite having no direction. I did not seek this happiness or expect it. It seemed to start oozing out of my pores one day. It continues to do so. I slowed the pace of my life, let go of attachments, and simply paid attention to what was going on. It seems to work. I see so many people in Korea and here in the West leading very sad but successful lives. What's more, the more successful they are, the sadder they seem to become. That's not me by a long shot.

I consciously chose to be unsuccessful. I had a good education and a confident personality, so it was not easy, but I stayed focused on my lack of gumption. Let others seek the corner office while I enjoyed the anonymity of the mail room. I drove a cab and a truck, though never at the same time. I refused promotions and shunned any new challenge that might lead to recognition. I argued for pay decreases to reflect my lack of commitment. I persevered. Today it has paid off, or rather it has not paid off, which was of course my objective in the first place. I think I proved that one can overcome a solid education and a winning personality without having to come out on top. I am a living testimonial of the undriven life.

25

Mindfulness is very popular these days. Not long ago it made the cover of Time magazine. More to the point the Library of Congress lists 4,063 titles that contain the word "mindful," including *Mindful Golf* and *Mindfulness and Murder*. And therein lies the rub. The word has been commodified and monetized to such an extent as to obliterate its original meaning.

The Pāli word for mindfulness is *sati*. As a practice, it is outlined in detail in the Satipaṭṭhāna Sutta, a talk given by the Buddha early in his teaching period. Mindfulness is almost always coupled with the idea of clear comprehension or wise understanding. Without this coupling component, a practitioner would simply be focusing their attention on something. This would relax the mind to an extent but would not lead to wisdom. If it could do so, then every tightrope walker would be enlightened, as would the best sharpshooters. The Buddha was more than a sideline coach asking you to "Get your head in the game," although you wouldn't know it from the books available at Amazon.

Understanding the practice as doing non-doing avoids many of these entanglements. As soon as you apply the practice to get better marks or improve your golf game, you are doing something, adding a kicker of craving to the original intent. Mindfulness devolves the ego by letting go of unskillful adopted behavior. Be wary of those who advocate any form of empowerment through mindfulness. Non-doing is not acquisitive. It is not a synonym for being the best you can be. The path does not empower strengths to make us better than others, it in fact disempowers the attitude that we must be better than others.

26

Trauma can exact a pernicious hold on our mind. Victims often seek help in the form of group therapy or individual counseling. Members of Alcoholics Anonymous admit to feeling helpless in the face of their inability to overcome their condition. They speak of themselves as survivors. They are to be commended for facing their trauma, seeing it for what it is. However, by not moving on, by replaying the trauma over and over, by self-identifying as trauma survivors, and by joining a movement of co-survivors, whatever relief they feel stems more from commiseration with others and a certain bequeathed status than from a letting go of or rising above the trauma. By so doing, they will remain forever tethered to this false identity and yoked to a mind state of "Why me?" Doing non-doing shifts the trauma from a personal tragedy to an understandable, conditioned response to a painful event.

Leo Tolstoy learned this lesson of reinforcing pain when he was just a mischievous young boy. His grandfather had grown exasperated at his failure to correct young Leo's behavior. A student of the mind, he decided to try a different tact one day after Leo had broken a vase. His grandfather told him to stand in the corner until he could stop thinking of "the white elephant." Leo was dumbfounded, for of course he had never in his young life given a thought to elephants, let alone white ones. He assumed he would be out of the corner within minutes. And so he commenced not thinking about "the white elephant." He tried very hard. He tried very hard all through lunch and well close to suppertime without success. The harder he tried to eliminate the thought and the more he desired to be free of the thought, the stickier it became. If he had

had access to this little book, he would have gained a whole day to continue to exasperate his grandfather. But then again, maybe he would never have produced *War and Peace*.

An old monk spent twenty years in a Chinese prison in Tibet, where he was tortured every day. Upon his release he made his way to India and met with the Dalai Lama, who asked him what the worst part of his incarceration had been. The old monk replied that while he was being beaten, he worried he might lose love for his torturers. He felt pain, but he suffered no trauma. He did not simply survive the torture. He lived it by remaining full of love, peace, and compassion.

27

My father fought in WW2. This entailed sleeping in drafty and cold English castles on camp cots, followed by living in bivouacs as the regiment made its way from Normandy up the coast to Arnhem in Holland. He suffered from chronic back pain the rest of his life. He had his throat slit by an enemy agent in London, and on a furlough was sexually assaulted. He never complained. Upon his return he married, had two children, and worked in the government. There he continued a life of quiet resolution, never missing a day of work. He did not think he was entitled to anything, neither for his service nor for the hardships he endured. He loved to golf but gave it up when he had a family. He had a job to do. He got on with life. He just swept what was in front of his broom.

My father was a Buddhist, though he didn't know it. One of the main tenets of the teachings of the Buddha is that "You alone are responsible for all your sorrows." No matter what pain or misery has visited you, it is entirely up to you how much you wallow in it or how much compensation, restitution, or special treatment you believe you are entitled to. Both these reactions will result in a further stirring of the pot of suffering. As Pema Chödrön points out, "The most difficult times for many of us are ones we give ourselves."

This is not to suggest that feelings of injustice or trauma or whatever strong emotions that continue replaying in your mind should be ignored or repressed. The feelings are natural results of being alive. They need to be acknowledged. However, the feelings are not a problem that *needs* to be healed. Suffering begins when you engage them, rolling in their meanderings as you replay once again the events of the past, augmenting their impact on different aspects of your life. By investing so much energy into past trauma, you are further conditioning the mind to react in similar ways to future trauma. You are pre-programming your mind for future misery.

Doing non-doing acknowledges these strong emotions, befriending them in a way. You can even call them by their name. "Oh look, sadness has arisen." You envelop the emotion with awareness. And with a calm abiding, by giving it lots of space. Your heart has plenty of room for family visitors and war-torn refugees alike. Every time you find yourself rolling in a memory, dialoguing with shoulds and could haves and next times, say hello to them and then bring yourself back to doing nothing about them.

28

In India they trap monkeys with a bamboo cage. The cage has a small opening just large enough for the monkey's hand to slip through. They slide a banana through the hole and wait. The monkey smells the banana and twists his hand through the hole and grabs the banana. Success. Or so he thinks, until he discovers that he can't extract his hand now that it is holding the banana. The hole is too small. He is trapped, but not by the cage. And not by the banana. He is trapped by his craving for the banana. To save his life all he needs do is drop the banana. He just has to let go.

And so do you. Doing non-doing involves a lot of letting go. In fact, letting go is a synonym for the doing part of doing non-doing. When you find you are holding on to what invariably is making you miserable, let it go. It may be familiar and somewhat comforting, it may even be healthy, but if your craving overwhelms your state of mind to the point of obsession, let it go. We are retraining the mind, and this can be frustrating work. Letting go of the banana may save this monkey (and you) this one time. But again, the banana is not the problem. The monkey and, more importantly, you, have to let your desire for the banana be. And in a way, even the desire is not the problem. Let the desire simply be a desire. It is a natural condition of the mind, arising and passing away on its own and in its own time. Watch it. Learn from its arising what craving feels like and learn from its passing away the wisdom of doing non-doing.

Craving is very subversive in that it deludes the mind into thinking that the object of the craving is very rational because only it can satisfy the gnawing in the pit of my stomach. This is all the more reasonable if my cohort is craving the same object. If everyone of my friends is craving a Maybach my mind then doesn't feel so unbalanced. "I am not crazy," you tell yourself. If this is the case, think back a few years to the Pokémon Go craze. This involved adults, many with very good jobs, families, and responsibilities going to great lengths, sometimes incurring life-threatening repercussions, in search of Pokémon characters that exist only online. You are trying to capture digitalized pixels, mere electronic pulsations, to elevate your status and happiness. Think this could not happen to you? Replace the words "digitalized pixels" in the previous sentence for whatever it is you are currently sacrificing your health, your time, or your money for to elevate your status or your pleasure. Now do you understand?

29

When the venerable Thai teacher, Ajahn Chah,was asked what technique of meditation he taught, he replied frankly, "I teach frustration." Doing non-doing can be in itself frustrating, but in the hands of a meditation master it can be nuclear.

Every day at around 5:00 pm, the Ajahn would meet with the monks and deliver a discourse, after which he would grant the monks permission to take a short break for tea. This tea break was the only sustenance they had to keep themselves going during the long evening meditation. The tea was heavily sugared and greatly anticipated.

One particular day after the Ajahn's discourse, he closed his eyes and meditated. The permission for tea was not forthcoming. The monks too closed their eyes and meditated as best they could under the circumstances. Most of them were frustrated at the delay of their much-anticipated tea. Still the Ajahn remained deep in meditation, seemingly impervious to the daily routine. This continued for a few hours, after which the monks realized no tea would be coming that day. They settled in for the long haul. Their frustration subsided. After a few more hours, Ajahn Chah opened his eyes and smiled. As did the monks. His silent discourse was over. It had been a very profound teaching. The Ajahn slowly arose and walked out of the hall, and the monks too left for their respective khutis, or small meditation huts.

The next day the few monks who had missed the discourse asked those who were there what the subject of the last evening's discourse was. Those who had attended remained silent. The other monks were confused by this non-response.

"I guess," they said, "you had to be there." Many years later they referred to this discourse as the best teaching Ajahn Chah had ever given without opening his mouth.

30

When you find yourself in a hole, first stop digging. Trite but true, when we find ourselves in this predicament, we need to lay down the activities that led us to be that deep in the hole. When I found myself in an alcohol-induced hole, I let all the alcohol-related activities go. These included for a time even good friends for whom weekend bacchanalia was the rule. I later added sporting events and music concerts to my list of abandoned habits, because without alcohol I simply found the noise excessive. Of course, I quickly felt better, more clearheaded, and more energetic. I started running. To run more efficiently, I switched to a plant-based diet. In those days there were very few vegetarian restaurants, so I spent a lot of my time cooking. And as I spent a lot of time recovering from my ever-longer runs, I spent more time reading. I was very comfortable with my more solitary life, because for the first time in many years I was not blindly following the leads of others. To better prepare my body for marathons, I took up yoga and for a while lived in an ashram in Pennsylvania. And shortly thereafter I went on my first meditation retreat. It was a natural progression, one thing leading in time to another. I had no fixed plan in mind. I simply began with an understanding that the *sine qua non* root cause of my discomfort was alcohol. Abstinence cleared my head, and everything after that followed naturally.

You can't stop digging if you don't realize you're in a hole. This inability to diagnose the problem can be exasperated if friends and family are all digging in the same hole. Even if you have a vague feeling that something is amiss, you can simply put the shovel down for a while and see how it feels. If you are under the spell of friends or family (as we all are to some extent), it might prove equally disastrous to climb out of that hole only to jump into another one. Anyone who has been cornered at a gathering by a recent convert to another religion or diet or hobby knows the danger of this well. The answer is not to be found in another hole.

To that point, another story. Some holy seekers came to the monastery for a teaching. The monk had tea served while they chatted. The monk stood and started to pour more tea into their already quite full cups. The tea spilled over the sides of the cups onto the floor. The seekers were perplexed. To spill tea was a very strange thing for a monk to do. The monk paused for a while to let the lesson sink in and then explained. "You can't add fresh tea to a cup that is already full."

31

I had an aunt who lived on a forty-acre estate west of Toronto. The manor house was an Elizabethan structure with separate breakfast and dining rooms, a full maid's quarters, apple orchards, and a forest with deer and other wildlife. In the late afternoon we would dress for tea and retire to the screened porch off the living room. My aunt would put Mozart on the hi-fi, and we would eat cucumber sandwiches. The tea service was Royal Doulton. Like a royal wedding, this scene could easily be misconstrued as pretentious and even haughty. Yet from the perspective of a twelve-year-old boy, the peace and tranquility of those summer afternoons spoke of a refined civility, devoid of rancor and ill will. I would not know such refined civility aside from the Royal Doulton until years later, when I would find it in abundance in the monasteries and temples of South and Southeast Asia. But it was at my Aunt's where the seed for a life of tranquil reflection in the company of like-minded individuals was first planted.

This is the thing about doing non-doing. You come to see more clearly how your mind was conditioned. And you see how you veered off track by ignoring subtle hints of what really made you happy. You dismissed those flashes of insight as not the real you anymore. You think you've moved on since then. You may even have been talked out of pursuing a different life by your family or your friends. Don't despair. These aha! moments, or better, these ah! moments planted seeds that have brought you to where you are now. These contented, happy moments of sublime perfection often occur during childhood because the mind isn't yet fully conditioned. But even if your childhood was lacking in these moments, they continue to manifest all around you. It is never too late to have a happy childhood.

32

An abscessed tooth forced me out of my hut and into Bombay, as it was known then, to see a dentist. I had his name on a piece of paper and was assured he was *ektampukkha,* "a cheap but best"dentist. No one was in the waiting room, and he said he could take me right away, two facts that should have warned me to be careful. Once I was in the chair, he quickly concluded my tooth was indeed abscessed and a root canal was in order. I gave him the go-ahead.

He gave me a glass of Dettol to swish around in my mouth. We didn't have time for antibiotics to work. Next, he told me he had no X-ray machine but was sure which tooth was the infected one from the pitch of my scream when he prodded my incisors with a sharp pick. Homework done, he started to drill. "Freezing?" I asked. He turned down the fan.

I had no choice but to watch the pain. I went to its very core. I analyzed it. Here it was less, there was its center, now the pain was sharp, now it was throbbing. When he began to saw the nerve, tears welled in my eyes, but I wasn't crying. Tearing up seemed to be my body's natural response to strong pain. It lasted no more than ten minutes, during which I had so much to watch, from the sensation of the tears rolling down my cheeks to the throbbing pain of the open cavity to the sharper pain of the saw, that the time passed quickly. He filled the cavity, and I was on my way.

A year or so later I was back in the West when the same tooth acted up. I saw a dentist who informed me the last root canal did not remove all the abscess. He'd have to do it again, though this time he took an X-ray, and more to the point, he froze the tooth. I didn't feel a thing. I was numb down to my toes. But I didn't learn anything. I came away from the non-experience no wiser than when I went in, proving that we learn more when we fall on our face than when we gaze at the stars.

33

A healthy component of the practice is to stay awake to encroaching spiritual materialism. This danger begins to raise its head after you think of yourself as an experienced practitioner. You may judge your practice as quite advanced. You pat yourself on the back. You start acquiring compliments. Thoughts that you might teach someday may flutter through your consciousness. Don't indulge in these meanderings. Keep an eye on them as you would a spot of crabgrass on an otherwise pristine lawn.

Like many Westerners, I fell hard for the local elixir of India: chai. The Brits introduced tea drinking as well as tea plantations centuries ago, but it took Indian ingenuity to perfect the correct ratio of tea, milk, and sugar, brew it up in huge vats, and sell it in miniscule mud cups which biodegraded after one rainfall and which sold for one rupee. Heaven. I soon got up to 20 cups a day and counting.

My chai addiction and I went on a thirty-day retreat. I decided to renounce chai for the entire time. Afterwards, I proudly announced to a friend how successful I was with my renunciation. "I really put my craving for chai in its place."

"I don't think so," he said. "Chai wasn't the problem. It was craving, and you simply toughed it out. There is nothing wrong with chai. You just don't know when to stop. You should have had one cup of chai every day, drank half of it, set it down, and walked away." Avoidance is a form of fleeing and as such is false renunciation. I was running away from facing up to my craving.

This wake-up call made me look at my life as a whole. I was a single guy at the time and celibate. When home in Canada,

I lived by myself in a very small apartment. There I created a cocoon of calm and quiet wherein confrontation and high-decibel interactions were kept at bay. I lived an insular life, convinced that my renunciation and forced ascetism were harbingers of imminent enlightenment. I was very proud of my ever-diminishing sense of self. I was indeed very proud to be the first one on my block to lose my ego. Ajahn Pasanno had my number when he remarked that "being comfortable is not the end of suffering."

~ 34

Nature doesn't lie. It acts according to natural laws. And human nature, too, doesn't lie. It plays out as a series of causes and effects. If the inputs are negative, stifling, abusive, or spiteful, the immediate effects may be unpleasant. Even if there is no evidence of any negative aftermath, in time, inauspicious acts invariably lead to a myriad of unintended and unforeseen negative circumstances. Rare is it to find a criminal who doesn't feel remorse about his deeds and who is not also suffering ten-fold due to substance abuse, turning as he would to drugs and alcohol to stem the remorse his crimes have precipitated.

Today it is equally rare is it to find someone who doesn't turn to his smartphone, his Facebook friends, his Twitter account, his video games in a seemingly endless search for likes and followers. Many seek positive reinforcement for every selfie on Instagram, to convince others but mostly themselves that they are indeed awesome. Everyone is complicit in this cacophony of lies, an endless and meaningless codependency. It is socially sanctioned addiction. To a greater or lesser extent, we are all trying to be someone else, someone constructed by other people's ideas of the top dog, or at least someone to envy.

That may sound a bit harsh, but I know of what I speak. Back in the day, I thought myself to be someone else. I wanted to be seen as a deep thinker, a student radical, a hippie philosopher king. I left home and moved into an apartment near the campus. I grew my hair into an unwashed urban jungle and began grad school in philosophy. I looked very deep. I hoped by dropping the names of Heidegger and Kierkegaard into every conversation and extolling the hidden meanings in the music of the Fugs and the films of Kurosawa that the girls would love me. My faux life lasted until it became too much for me to maintain this façade. I had a breakdown of sorts, but fortunately I understood in a flash that I was an artist performing a role of someone else's ideal life. This was exhausting. Life is hard enough without trying to be someone else living it. As Charles Horton Cooley observed a century ago, "I am not what I think I am, and I am not what you think I am. I am what I think you think I am."

So I cut my hair, moved back home, and dropped out of school. I wasn't cool anymore, but I wasn't anyone else either. I was back to being a boring nerd who still lived with his parents. But this was a good place to rest a while until my next step became clear.

Lay your burden down. There is no salvation out there. There is not even a there there. Remember that as the Stoics noted the wise man is content within himself.

35

For my father's entire life, I was not a parent. In his presence I reverted to a child-like sense of entitlement. His world revolved around me and this, I thought, was how it should be. I had my family after he had passed away. And it was only as my boys got older and I dealt with all the practical aspects of child-rearing that I fully appreciated all my father had done. I loved him all the more and grieved his passing with every crisis my wife and I faced.

Every time I stayed up all night with one of our sons, I thought my father must have done the same. When my youngest fell on his head and I spent the day checking the dilation of his pupils until he thought I was a lighthouse and he would run away each time I reached for a flashlight, I thought of my father taking me to the hospital for a suspected broken finger late at night. I realized he must have loved me that much as well. And when one son got a sticky for sitting in his cubby on the first day of school or my other son won two academic awards when he passed into high school, I was flushed with pride, just as my father must have been when I won the senior spelling bee when I was only a junior. (As I write this, I use spell check, and I can hear him saying, "Come on, son, spell like a man!" in his full-on, "get-out-of-the-foxhole-soldier" sergeant-major voice.) And every time I drive my sons to a basketball game or a birthday party, I think of my father getting up Saturday mornings, sometimes as early as 5:00 am, to get me to a hockey game on a freezing outdoor rink. He was our coach, and he stood out there with us in a thin woolen coat and leather shoes.

My father was very taciturn, a man of few words and the many demands to be a real man. He never spanked me, and he never hugged me. I waited until late in his life to tell him I loved him. I am glad I did, but it was only recently that I realized why I loved him so much. I raise my sons in the only way I know how because I learned from the best. Like my father did, I may not always sound like it, but I too act out of love because I have no choice.

36

One night a man lost his keys. He looked for them under a street lamp. A friend walked by, saw him looking for something, and asked him what he lost.

"My keys," he replied.

"Oh," said his friend. "Where did you lose them?"

"Over there. In the woods," came the reply.

Stunned, the friend asked, "But why are you looking for them here?"

"The light is much brighter here!" the man replied.

This is the mistake we keep making over and over again. We think the answer to why we feel miserable can only be found under the bright lights where we find the shiny 10,000 things. It just seems to make so much sense. Besides, everyone else seems to be there. They seem euphoric, and for some of them it was as simple as switching to a new toothpaste! The shiny 10,000 things look so compelling that surely they must be the answer to what seems to be ailing me. They will fill my life with joy and happiness.

We all suffer from this delusion of cognitive dissonance, much as Nazrudin did in a teaching centuries ago. He was eating hot chilies one after the other, crying uncontrollably due to the ulcers in his mouth. When asked why he continued to eat the chilies, he replied, "I am trying to find a sweet one." Impossible, you say. Sweetness is not a property of chilies. Precisely. Nor is happiness or fulfillment or status a property of anything, no matter how shiny or well-presented that thing may be.

The 10,000 things are bound to disappoint. But your habit patterns are such that you persistently keep looking under the bright lights. You are mesmerized by the neon glitter, the buzz of category 5 excitement, the OMG breathless reporting of the galas and festivals. All are devoid of any substantive happiness DNA. "Maybe this time?" you think despite constant disappointment. A recent survey of hundreds of thousands of urbanites (Toronto, Vancouver, etc.) told a tale of profound loneliness, mind-numbing commutes, unaffordable housing, and a general malaise due to a lack of connectedness. But the lights…oh how they shine! People from all over the world are flocking to the big cities with the hope that they may grab the gold ring.

And so 2,500 years ago, the Buddha set out on a quest. In modern parlance, he wanted to know why the human mind is hardwired to make irrational decisions over and over again.

37

The Buddha was more scientist than spiritual seeker. He wanted to understand human suffering using himself, his body, and his mind as his laboratory. After many years of ascetic practices, while sitting under a pipal tree in Bihar in northern India, he took a vow not to move until his experiment gave up an answer. As dawn broke so did the yoke that tied him to this earthly realm. Enlightenment. He was now awakened. He was now the Buddha. The one who knows. And what does he ask of us? Reverence? Obedience? Blind devotion? Not at all. He asks you to come and see for yourself.

He would continue to teach, giving 84,000 discourses over the ensuing forty-five years covering his main, perhaps singular, theme: suffering and the end of suffering. He provided the details behind the mind's thought processes that cause the suffering, and he did so in a way that his audience would easily grasp the science behind the path.

The first stage in thinking, he explained, is consciousness. I am aware of what I am seeing (or hearing, feeling, smelling, or tasting), usually its shape, size, color. For the sake of clarity, let's say I am conscious of a yellow, cylindrical object. This first stage is bare cognition. The second stage, arising a nanosecond after the first stage, is perception or recognition. "Ah, it's a banana." The mind is working fine. The object is familiar, and now it has a name.

Again, almost simultaneously with recognition of this yellow, cylindrical object called a banana, comes the third stage, when my conditioning begins to rev its engines. Here a plethora of physical and mental feelings, all intertwined and cross referencing, neurotransmitters lighting up like a pinball game in an arcade, hijack my original, conscious recognition of an object and take it on a blind roller-coaster ride that jumps the tracks, turns upside down, and dumps me in a dodgy part of town. I not only don't know where I am, but it all occurred so quickly, I don't know how I got there. I am awash with negative or positive sensations and emotions. All this from seeing a mere banana! And I'm not done yet. Call this stage "sensations." It is an emotional reaction, based on conditioning, to what right now my mind is dealing with, which in this case is still just a banana.

In the final stage of the process, I react to this wild goose chase of sensations and emotions either with warm, fuzzy, pleasant feelings that make me feel good or sharp, almost painfully upsetting, feelings that make me feel badly or occasionally not feel strongly one way or the other, probably because I am confused. These four stages of mind propel me to act as I am wont to do under these particular circumstances. Through all four stages, "I" was absent. I didn't go out of my way to realize the yellow thing was a banana. It occurred spontaneously with seeing the object. And more importantly, I didn't choose to rev up any engines, hijack anything, or take a roller-coaster or a taxi to the dodgy part of town. It's obvious I am not the director of my own movie. This is so much so that Yongey Mingyur Rinpoche observes, "most people simply mistake the habitually formed, neuronally constructed image of themselves for who and what they really are."

When asked to sum up the teaching in one sentence, the Buddha's primary disciple, Śāriputra, answered, "In seeing, just see." Ajahn Sumedho paraphrases and asks us to "observe our habitual tendencies as conditions that arise and cease. In this state, the repressed fears and emotional states can rise up… [and] reach the surface." Now I too can see and feel them and understand how they condition all my thinking and behavior.

By doing non-doing, by not giving in to exhortations to act, these habitual reactions eventually cease or at least quiet down. We then can catch a glimpse of the unconditioned mind, pure consciousness in its natural state.

38

The Buddha was more than an enlightened teacher, he was also the first neuroscientist. He confirmed neuroplasticity, the mind's ability to change by restructuring itself at the neurological level. The Buddha altered his mind to such an extent that he transcended the final two complex, problematic stages of the thinking process. He declared himself enlightened, which is to say free from the shackles of greed, hatred, and delusion. This was proof positive, as James Olds, a professor of neuroscience, said, that the mind is not just plastic but "very plastic." So much so that from then on, in seeing, the Buddha could just see.

The Buddha's discovery had to wait almost 2,500 years for confirmation from the scientific community. Up to that point, the mind was seen as a fixed entity. This changed when Michael Merzenich, at the University of Wisconsin in 1968, scrambled the brain map of monkeys by severing a nerve in their hands. The monkeys were of course very confused at first. But when he returned to the experiment a few months later, he discovered that the neural pathways had rewoven themselves into a new map that reflected the new arrangement of the nerves in their hand. The Buddha was right. Doing non-doing repatterns the old neurotransmitters and creates new pathways which reprogram the way the mind sees the world.

Michael Greenberg observed that our neurological system is "an ephemeral place that changes as our experience changes." Doing non-doing brings awareness and equanimity to old habit patterns, tilting the mind towards awakening and away from habitual, sometimes destructive, patterns.

Neuroplasticity proves that the more we repeat a thought or an action, the more we continue exercising and growing the circuits they formed. This is the neurological basis for our addictions and our more subtle habits, positive and negative. It is particularly problematic with predispositions like depression and OCD. The more we concentrate on our symptoms, the deeper those symptoms become etched onto our minds. The mind can become what it fears it may, or already may have, become. It is held hostage by old habits. Focusing on them to try to eliminate or heal them by sheer will or through intervention, divine or otherwise, or indulging in them out of helplessness reinforces the old habits. The only way out is through, and the only way through is to do nothing.

By repeating "new" patterns like awareness and equanimity, the mind develops positive neurotransmitters. This is the reason a daily meditation practice is so necessary. And if the word "practice" is off-putting, then think of it as developing a craft, from the German *kraft*, which means, "a power that comes from understanding." Doing non-doing is indeed a wise way to see things as they really are. And in the process, uncovering the unconditioned being that was already there.

Old habits die hard. The practice proceeds at a snail's pace and yet it feels good to be heading in a new direction. I remember feeling calmer and more contented simply because I was no longer living a lie because it proved too difficult to keep track of all my alter egos. What I was uncovering may not have been pretty, may have been full of contradictions, and was quite often a disappointment. But it was also a relief to see into and chip away at the façade of "me." No more pretending. Once I uncovered more of my real being, I realized all the myriad micro-lies I had been telling myself to keep the façade going. It was only by stepping back from the habit of pretending what others wanted to see in me that I became aware of the true heaviness of carrying around my faux creations.

39

My father would go apoplectic when he was near gum chewers. He would physically recoil as they mashed away in complete obliviousness to the consternation they were causing him. Though I didn't understand the reason for his meltdowns, over time I absorbed his attitude. Each time some unsuspecting gum smacker tried to engage my father in a conversation, I could feel my father do a slow burn. Like a tuning fork hearing a note played on a piano, I would commiserate with him, and my habit patterning would be dug a tad deeper.

Not only do I react with revulsion should someone chew gum as they talk to me, but I imbibe the perpetrators of such ignorance with the smug moniker of being singly responsible for the death of Western civilization as we know it. Today, of course, I do nothing about these old habit patterns, and over time they have quieted, and I say nothing, but old habits are such that even their dying embers can cast off heat.

I have impressionable children of my own, and I have consciously chosen not to comment on the decibel levels of their chewing. Nor do I comment on other people's eating habits in their presence. Lo and behold, when my lovely Korean wife SLURPS her Korean noodles (as she was taught to do by her parents) my boys barely flinch. They join her in a virtual slurpathon. Everyone continues eating, despite producing noises registering in the triple figures on the Richter scale and causing goodness knows how many tsunamis off the coasts of a few Polynesian islands. I do not react. I say nothing. My wife and children remain free of mastication judgment that has troubled our family for goodness knows how many generations. It stopped with me. However, during the evening slurpathon,

I sometimes quietly take my bowl of noodles and retire to the den downstairs to do some deep breathing. Enough is enough for goodness' sake.

40

"You've got to learn your instrument. Then, you practice, practice, practice. And then, when you finally get up there on the bandstand, forget all that and just wail." This was the great jazz saxophonist, Charlie Parker's, musical lesson. But it could as well have been the Buddha's advice. You've got to understand the mind. Then you've got to practice that way of seeing. And then when doing non-doing is firmly established, you can forget all that and just wail. Okay, maybe the Buddha wouldn't have talked about just wailing, but as a metaphor for just being, I think Charlie was on the right track.

Practice stretches a singular blip of awareness into two blips and eventually into a continuous stream of insight into the mind's machinations. But for even that singular moment of unconditioned awareness of one breath or some pain in your knee or a troubling thought, you are a Buddha. For that one moment in which you are aware and yet calmly abiding whatever is going on, you are enlightened. And you will understand that doing non-doing isn't such an unattainable big deal. You just have to string these individual blips into a stream. And for this, you have to practice. In Zen, the metaphor is that "there is no end to practice and no beginning to enlightenment."

Michael Jordan took 1,000 shots every day of his career. In any match when he found himself off his game, he didn't panic. His inner core remained strong and confident because he had done the hard work in the gym day after day. He would go back to the basics, not overthinking his shots and not trying too hard. And soon his game would come back, and like Charlie, he could just wail.

After many decades of practice, I have days where my concentration wanes, my focus is off, or I am beset by one or more of the many negative mind states. At such times I forget about wailing, and I return to the basics. I observe my breath or focus on external noises or on the throbbing in my knee, anything to hang my hat on until the mind settles down, the negative mind states quiet, and slowly and ever so quietly, I begin to wail.

41

You need to walk before you run. This much is certain. There is an old joke of a tourist lost in New York City who asked a passerby how to get to Carnegie Hall. He was told, "Practice, my boy, practice." This process can appear to be slow going. This is quite normal, as the progress is incremental. (And meditation practice redefines incremental.) It can seem at times to be "one step forward and two steps back!" There is a temptation to speed up the work, perhaps through ever longer and longer retreats, moving to India, or seeking out secret teachings from every guru who passes through town. This too is another form of spiritual materialism, the meditative equivalent of the saying that if a Mercedes Benz is a good car, then two are even better.

A novice was walking beside the river when he spotted his Master on the other side. Not seeing any bridge, he shouted across, "Master, how do I get to the other side?"

To which the Master replied, "You ARE on the other side."

The truth does not reside in an isolated Himalayan cave. Nor can it be found in this book or in a particularly holy teacher. The truth resides within you, albeit somewhat hidden beneath a rotting pile of self-reinforcing habit patterns. But as the story above so succinctly informs us, there is nowhere you need to go. You are already where you need to be. You are indeed already on the other side. You need not change your job or your partner. You need not put on robes or shave your head. You need not take a vow of silence. You don't need to go by one name. Again, it was Marcus Aurelius who pointed out that "No other life is more appropriate for the practice of philosophy than that which you happen to be living."

There is nowhere to go. And nothing to do. Literally. Nothing to do.

42

In large stores in Korea there is a greeter at the front door. He or she bows and wishes you well and a good shopping experience. Koreans are used to this formal welcome. They walk by without so much as a by-your-leave. I am, however, quite taken with obsequiousness. If you want my attention, bow. I find it just so polite. A little groveling is good for the soul, as my mother used to say. So, I feel I should acknowledge their good wishes. But by the time I formulate a response and make sure it is a Korean one, the greeter has moved on and is addressing the couple behind me. They don't really hear his greeting. For them he is white noise. But me they hear. Perhaps it is my accent. Or maybe that I'm saying hello in Hindi. Whatever the reason, they turn their heads and look at me. Then they look at each other as if to say, "Who is he talking to? Should we know him?"

43

The question remains, however, why is practice so difficult?

To begin with, doing non-doing is by and of itself difficult because to be still and just watch goes against our very nature. This is especially true when the objects of our gaze may be as exciting as drying paint. And sometimes the difficulty lies with the other extreme, as when we are confronted with something quite painful. But, joy of joys, there are quite a few more reasons it is difficult. And they present themselves in the form of impediments, mind states so devious and insidious that they kidnap all your hard-earned attention and seem to cast it into the deepest dungeon in the castle and throw away the key.

The first two impediments can be talked about together: our old friends, greed and hatred. In this guise they are like young children suffering from the terrible "no's." Greed wants to be anywhere and doing anything but sitting alone quietly. Or it sidetracks you into false illusions, that you love the last person you saw at the supermarket or that you really need a dog. It is irrational craving…squared. Greed's flipside, hatred, is strong aversion for someone or something that may have bothered you years or even decades ago. It could be a bit of unfinished business, but it crops up now because the mind is relatively calm, and hatred doesn't like calm, so it flashes images at you to knock you off your new game of composed abiding.

The third trickster is sloth or torpor. You got a good night's sleep, but as soon as you close your eyes while sitting on your cushion you feel engulfed in a warm infusion of sleep-inducing mist.

Fourth is worry or anxiety, those two guards at the door who have kept humankind alive and safe since the Pleistocene era.

Worry placed a guard at the entrance to the cave, just in case a sabretooth tiger stopped by for a late-night snack. Worry is just so justified. For instance, what if…and away you go for the next twenty minutes into the rocky land of possibility which is found only two "what if's" past the Elysian fields of probability.

And finally, there is doubt casting its dark cloud over your practice and questioning all the gains you've made over the past few days or years or decades. It opens up a bottomless pit of internal dialogue that concludes nothing. It's doubt, after all, not reason. Doubt bows to nothing.

The solution to these pernicious intruders is to call them by their name, like in a game of hide-and-seek: "I see you, Billy." As well, don't linger on the object of their attention. Usually they will sidetrack you all the more when they hook their greed onto Beyoncé or their hatred onto Donald Trump. Keep it at the level of the impediment. "I see you, greed." Thirdly use the time these impediments are in the forefront of the mind to practice calm abiding and simply wait them out. Too much effort to eradicate them only strengthens them. Remember, you've got all the time in the world, so don't waste a minute of it.

44

Happiness is not something to pursue. Like the truth, happiness too is not out there somewhere. Chasing it is like a dog trying to catch its tail. Happiness has been hijacked by old habit patterns which have convinced us to look for it under the bright lights. We are so busy frantically seeking it here, there, everywhere that our ensuing agitation obscures the fact that happiness is right in front of us. Happiness is a great problem only when we try to solve it and eludes us only when we search for it. We just need to pay attention. We need to wake up. We need to see reality within and without ourselves in a new unfettered way. As in the following old tale…

Nazrudin was a poor but very clever merchant. Every day he would bring his goods on the back of donkeys across the border into the adjoining country to sell. Day after day. The border guards were sure he was smuggling something into their country, but search as they might, they could never find any contraband. Eventually he retired.

One day enjoying a coffee in a café, he bumped into one of the border guards, himself now retired. The border guard spoke to Nazrudin. "We are both retired now. I no longer have any power to arrest you. But I am curious. What were you smuggling all those years?"

Replied Nazrudin with a smile, "Donkeys."

A psychological experiment proved this very point. Subjects were asked to watch a video of two groups of ten athletes separated by an open space. One group was dressed in white and used a black ball. The other group was dressed in black and used a white ball. The subjects were asked to count the number of passes each team made. Almost all of the subjects had perfect scores. Then each was asked if they had seen the gorilla in the space between the teams. A gorilla! None had seen it. So the psychologists replayed the tape. This time they did not have to count the number of passes, and sure enough there in the space between the two teams arrived a full-sized gorilla who beat his chest and did other gorilla-like actions before disappearing. It was right in front of them, but the subjects were too busy looking elsewhere. They were looking, they just weren't seeing.

An older fish swims by two minnows and asks, "How's the water, boys?" The two minnows look at each other and ask, "What's water?"

Donkeys. Water. The nose on the front of your face. The truth. Happiness. All right in front of you. Stop looking where it isn't. And then stop looking for it where it might be. And finally, even stop looking for it inside, where the Buddha said it resides. Once you give up fully, you understand wherever it resides it is the search that holds it at bay.

45

Without the ability to silently sit alone in a darkened room, we are destined to be a slave to our conditioned mind, reacting to self-imposed habitual preconditions, convinced that everything out there is awesome and everyone else is as happy as kings. So why, you wonder, am I so miserable? I have lost count of the number of times in a given day I start a sentence with the plea "if only…"

This treatise is an invitation to wake up and see clearly. If you see the truth, you will understand the truth, and then you can practice the truth. If you practice the truth, then you will see the truth, and then you will understand the truth. If you understand the truth, then you will practice the truth, and then you will see the truth. It is described as a path only because we must use words which by their nature come in a sequential order, one after the other, implying a first-this-then-that approach to any teaching. The truth more resembles a wheel than a path. And the wheel rolls properly when every spoke bears an equal responsibility, with neither a first spoke nor an ultimate one.

When you understand the mind in the right way, meditation or doing non-doing becomes more than an interesting option. It becomes a vital necessity. Nothing in our external environment may change, but we see it and even feel it at a visceral level in a newly unconditioned way. We may see clearly that we really are happy working on Wall Street augmenting the investments of our clients. Everything may remain the same, except for everything being different. The flowers in the garden of my familiar world appear to bloom a tad brighter when unencumbered by weeds of conditioning. James Oppenheimer notes that "The foolish man seeks happiness in the distance.

The wise grows it under his feet." Clear the weeds from your garden first before entertaining the need to move to a better garden with a better climate.

Remaining awake is to be fully alive. For too long a time, I lived in a fog of confusion, sleepwalking through my days; now I tune into the simple joy of being alive. And sometimes just to be alive to the yin and the yang is sufficient. Who knows what discovery or insight or other serendipitous event might occur on a simple outing to buy socks. Or as Walt Whitman observed later in his life, "I have perceived that to be with those I like is enough."

46

For many years I faithfully sat two hours a day. This was my formal meditation practice. Two hours a day is a lot of meditation, I thought. I was wrong. Two hours a day is a lot of practice, but it is not a lot of meditation. Meditation cannot be measured. It can't be quantified in terms of time. Doing non-doing is a way of seeing, an understanding or insight, into the reality of each moment. It is not on a scale. It has no beginning and no end. There is no start time and no finishing time.

I once asked Ajahn Viradhammo if he had a formal sitting practice. He said he didn't, but he meditated all the time. Exactly. If you are always doing non-doing while you go about the business of life, there really is no need to set aside a prescribed period to do non-doing. It would be like a fish practicing swimming a few hours a day.

This became evident to me with the birth of my first child. As any parent can attest, a young baby requires 24-hour care. I would help out my wife whenever I could so she could get some rest. The rest of my day was spent changing and washing diapers, preparing meals, etc. I had little time for formal sitting, and when I did get to my cushion, I invariably fell asleep. What to do but make washing and cleaning and chopping carrots my practice? I realized quite quickly that this moment-to-moment awareness was not an alternative to the path. It was the path. Formal practice was a warm-up, a daily refresher, a honing of my awareness, necessary, no doubt, but not the be-all and the end-all by itself. Yes, you need to practice, but don't forget your daily wail.

Doing non-doing will become the new normal. In time, almost every waking moment will be infused with understanding and clear comprehension. Just as naturally, attention will focus on the act at hand, whether washing the dishes, cleaning, making the bed, getting dressed, shaving, etc. Everything heretofore thought to be so mundane as to almost necessitate idle speculation can be an act worthy of focus and clear comprehension.

I have tea every day. This is a wonderful opportunity to see with clear comprehension. There is the boiling of the water and the preheating of the pot and the cups. The tea is measured carefully, steeped for precisely four minutes, poured, and served. All with awareness. All with clear comprehension. This state of mind continues into the drinking of the tea and the ensuing conversation. I think we misunderstand the Japanese tea ceremony when we think it implies it is done very stiffly. It is not. It is formal, yes, but not from rote learning. Nothing is being done. It is a ritual, yes, but not a performance, undertaken with awareness and quiet probity. Precisely what is being poured? Tea? Of course it is, but I think one could argue that what is being poured is calm insight into a daily, mundane activity. And if this can be true for tea why not for washing the dishes? Why not for making the bed? Why not for…

47

We used to drive to Toronto every Christmas vacation to spend the holidays with my grandmother. It was about 250 miles away, two-lane blacktop all the way. Our means of conveyance was at first a Prefect and later a Vanguard, both inexpensive, four-cylinder British imports with all the fire power of a lawn mower with Chronic Fatigue Syndrome.

My father called all his cars "Caesar," after Julius, not Syd. This was the name of his father's horse, a particularly stubborn and finickity beast of burden. Since my father was knee-high to a grasshopper, he had heard exonerations to Caesar to get moving. Both British imports had a choke to modify the flow of gas to the carburetor. Set it too low and Caesar would remain immobile except for the odd bit of flatulence from its rear end. Set it too high and it flooded, requiring a ten-minute wait while Caesar pouted. This was particularly true during the Canadian Christmas season. Other families sang Christmas carols as they travelled. We swore along with my father urging Caesar to keep us going.

My father measured every trip in laps as if we were Emil Zatopek running the ten thousand meters. He did this to keep my sister and me from asking him, "How much longer?" every five minutes. The Universal Law of Travel with Minors declares that the number of times said question is asked is in inverse portion with the age of the children. And of course, every trip to Toronto consisted of a different number of laps.

The best part of the trip was lunch at the Rock Haven Hotel in Peterborough at about the halfway marker. This was our yearly meal out of the home, where I discovered the meaning of the word "taste." I always ordered the same thing: a chocolate milkshake, a hamburger, and French fries. I did not speak during the meal. I had waited a whole year for this. I minded my P's and Q's. I was not going to give my father any excuse to swear that "Next year it's Spam sandwiches in the car!" I wanted all his anger to remain focused on Caesar.

48

The fourth and final noble truth, the prescription for our illness, to continue the medical metaphor, is outlined in eight stages. The path (which is not, you may remember, a path but a wheel) covers everything from your behavior, your occupation, your speech, and your daily practice, right up to your thoughts and understanding. Note, however, this is not a moral edict from some God outlawing certain actions and behaviors as sinful. Nor does it demand altruistic acts to gain some kind of reward.

The Buddha provided the antidote for suffering. His stages outline acts and behaviors and views that facilitate enlightenment based on his own empirical discoveries. Acts and behaviors and views that contravene these stages lead to increased misery. The choice is yours. If you choose to follow the path, you are asked to accentuate those acts and behaviors and views that are deemed by empirical experience as conducive to enlightenment and avoid as best you can those acts and behaviors and views that are conducive to misery. There is no divine retribution for failing to do so. You dust yourself off and start again, just as the old Japanese proverb encourages us to "Fall down seven times, get up eight."

The Buddha was a man, not a god. He searched for the cause and the antidote of misery. His very life and his own mind were his lab. After an arduous, decade-long search, during which time he almost died, he succeeded. He spent the rest of his life teaching the good news to groups small and large throughout the Gangetic plains. He made clear that he cared not a jot if you listened to his talk and agreed with him. He expected you to prove the truth of what he said yourself. For 2,500 years, millions of people have followed and benefited from his teachings. Today his teachings are more popular than ever before. Almost every country in the world has its own temples, monasteries, and meditation centers. Scientists are studying the minds of experienced meditators, and neuroscientists are concluding that the Buddha's teachings reveal truths that they themselves are just today corroborating. People who practice the teachings are benefiting from a new way of seeing. Think of how successful the Buddha would have been if he had had God on his side!

49

Doing non-doing, allowing the suffocating angst in, though insisting it must sit in the corner and not suck out all the oxygen in the room, opens up a new way of seeing and experiencing daily life. It is as if you had been suffering from severe cataracts before and now your vision is unimpaired. The clouds have dissipated. The familiar takes on subtle hues and an unfamiliar clarity, leading one to marvel in the contradiction that while everything is the same, everything is different.

This new way of seeing and experiencing is one of the corollaries of the practice. It inspires you to keep on the path and even double up your efforts. This new way of seeing is a signpost along the way that assures you that as far as you have gone the teachings have been correct.

I went for a run every morning when I lived outside Jeju city on the eponymous Korean island. It seemed it was always raining. I liked the winding country roads bordered by low walls of volcanic rocks. My running schedule was such that I invariably would pass young girls on their way to school. Korean men don't run, so even from a distance they knew I was *gaijing*. This gave them time to prepare to say something to me. Usually it was, "Good morning, Mr. Jones," which they had learned in school. Then they would giggle. I always answered them. I liked to let them know I understood them. I didn't mind that they got my name wrong. Mostly, I just liked to hear them giggle in the rain.

These kinds of encounters, the miracles of small things, present themselves daily. They are like leprechauns—omnipresent, yes, but only seen by the quiet ones who are open to mystical beings. The unconditioned mind provides the compost from which the miracles of small things grow in our consciousness, wonder arising even on rainy days, arriving often with the musical accompaniment of children giggling.

50

I run almost every day. I don't push myself. I enjoy the sights and especially the smells as I run. I don't wear my glasses for that reason; my astigmatism enhances my sense of smell. I like the mustiness of mud thawing in the early spring and the tang of last night's rain as it evaporates in the first rays of the sun. Running is a kind of physical meditation. I am hyperaware of my breathing and every tweak and twitch in my body. I feel the sensations in my footfall. Like my daily meditation practice, I do it without a goal in my mind. I am unconcerned about my times or the number of miles I cover. I leave the results to the *Dhamma* (Sanskrit *Dharma*). At one time, I was a Type A runner, keeping a running journal, setting goals, and collecting memorabilia from different races. My more relaxed attitude coincided with the birth of my children.

Years ago, if I could, I would leave my house at first light. As I get older, each sunrise lays its claim as the greatest miracle in history. If I did run at daybreak, my family would still be asleep. When I returned, I would look in on each of them. When my youngest was still on the breast, my wife required a few more hours of sleep. He slept beside her on the futon, though he would kick off his part of the blanket. Most mornings he would remain on the bed. This alone was a small miracle. Sometimes I would find him upside-down and on the floor. He was too young to sleepwalk, but he could sleeproll with the best of them.

His older brother slept the sleep of the gods, as my mother used to say. I don't know what that means, but I do agree that if the gods slept, they would look like him in the morning light. A sight for sore eyes, also as my mother used to say. One morning I stared at him for a long time and realized I was wrong about what constitutes a miracle. As miracles go, the sunrise came a distant second.

The miracles of small things are right in front of us, right now. Our overly busy, always doing conditioned mind steers us in the direction of perceived emergencies, drawing our attention away from seeing all the miracles in front of us. Yes, sometimes the miracles are otherworldly and celestial, but more often than not they are right under our feet, like an upside-down baby on the floor. We see more often when we stoop than when we soar, nurturing something Ajahn Chah called, "earthworm knowledge."

51

Even the daily grind can be seen anew. Marcus Aurelius said it best: "Early in the morning I am rising to do the work of a human being." It matters not a jot how you spend your days, but each one bears the possibility of doing the work of a human being.

Korea is a land of entrepreneurs. Many set up kiosks along the sidewalk, selling everything from soup to nuts. For almost two hours one day, I watched one kiosk which sold leather belts and duct tape. The owner sat in the sun on the steps of the coffee shop in front of his kiosk. He would banter with the tofu seller in the next kiosk and flirt with the older women who paused to look at his wares. He engaged with almost everyone, and he would laugh a lot. As he interacted with people he'd unpack and repackage various things for easy sale. The whole time I watched him he did not make a sale—not a very good businessman. Newer or even just different products never appeared in his stall. Not a very good businessman, but certainly in the right business. Perhaps for him his kiosk was part of his spiritual practice, contributing to the Gross Domestic Happiness.

Another story. An old man collected the newspapers left by commuters on the Seoul subway. All day he traveled the different lines until he met his quota. He would be paid so many won per kilogram at the recycling depot. He probably got enough for a meal of rice and kimchee. This would be his only meal of the day. As he passed me one morning on the subway, he looked up at me. He patted his collection and said in English, "Newspapers." I raised my eyes in exclamation and mouthed, "Wow!" He smiled at me, and I smiled at a job well done. He collected a few more discarded newspapers. I glanced at the other passengers, mostly businessmen and government workers. He remained the only one smiling.

52

Life naturally simplifies. The many miracles of small things sidetrack the singular quest for ever greater success and accomplishments. Life loses its Photoshop luster when you simply live it. The little voices in your head or your gut may tell you to go right or left, here or there as they are conditioned. These are not usually the voices of wisdom but of past blind and dubious reactions that continue to condition the mind.

I traveled a lot, even after my wife and I had our sons. I never bought a Lonely Planet guide. I did not seek out any advice of what to see or where to go in any country. I liked to pluck myself down into some place and settle in for a while. I'd scout out a local market and some café where I could get a decent cup of tea. Anything more would just get in the way.

I did not do much most days, for instance. Not doing much was okay, especially when we lived in Korea. I knew where the market was, and they knew me at the local tea house. I was a foreigner but not a tourist. If I were, I would feel obligated to visit a palace or a traditional village. I was not under any such pressure. I was free to get on with my life. I'd shop for vegetables. I'd go for a cup of coffee. I'd buy some socks. I was glad I was not a tourist. When you're a tourist you have to go to a palace. You never get to buy new socks.

I agree with Tolkien that "not all those who wander are lost." You can only be lost if you are following a map.

53

Many years ago, I attended a performance of Aida. This was a full production and the director wanted to impress. In the opening scene, he featured a live elephant. The audience seemed to anticipate the arrival of the elephant more than the two hours of Verdi that would follow the pachyderm's entrance. As the curtain parted, there stood the elephant as right as rain, center stage. The woman seated beside me, unable to contain herself, shouted, "Oh look! An elephant!" I am proud to say I didn't shout out, "Where?" Talk about the elephant in the room!

I was reminded of that moment every time I took the Seoul subway. Before the subway arrived, there would be a huge gush of wind down the tunnel pushed forward by the coming train. The train's front light then would be seen coming down the track. When the train stopped, there would be a loud ringing that announced the doors had now been opened. A herd of passengers exited the train. At that moment, an electronic sign flashed the ground-breaking news, "The train has arrived." Thank you. At first, I thought it was an elephant.

See. Just see, be awake to the very miracle of being awake at this moment and see what is in front of you. You don't need an internal baseball analyst telling you what it is you are looking at. Nor do you have to capture the scene on your cell. When you are awake to the ebb and flow of life as a natural unfolding, a being-here-now quality is always present. In Zen this is called emptiness. This is not nothing. This is a state of pure awareness, devoid of my bombastic ego intervening, bringing the wrath of its whole editorial department down on me, judging, posturing, comparing, fearing, and craving, all the while keeping the miracles of small things at bay.

See without knowing, or rather, without having to know. Why do you need to know what you see? Is a sunset more mesmerizing because I know what it is? Is a crime less brutal, knowing it contravenes a certain legal statute? Why do you need to decide whether the object of your attention is beautiful or not? Why can't seeing, hearing, tasting, smelling, and touching just be? These are not questions that demand answers as much as they require our attention. Pema Chödrön advises us to "Appreciate everything, even the ordinary... especially the ordinary."

~ 54

When I was young, I would spend a few weeks of my summer holiday at my grandmother's in Toronto. She lived by herself in a small apartment in the downtown. She had no television. She had no games or toys. There were no books at my age level, let alone comics. I loved it. My mother would catch up with Grandma. I was left to fend for myself. I was totally free, unprogrammed, unentrapped. I counted cars. I ran the streets. I could travel the subway all day for five cents. The museum up the street was free. I set my own agenda. It was a very simple time, boring, even, and repetitive, no doubt. But the freedom was intoxicating.

I watched my sons when we were in Asia. They were experiencing that same freedom. We had no plans, no commitments, no agenda, and no money. Poverty stimulates resourcefulness, so they played with whatever they found at the end of their hands. Cardboard boxes that were rockets the day before became caves the next. Going up to Grandma's at night in their pajamas was a great adventure. They'd press noses to the windows during bus and subway rides, not wanting to miss anything. When a train passed us going in the opposite direction, my oldest alerted his fellow passengers, "Look! A train!" This news bulleting seldom caused anyone to look up from their cell phones. They were impervious to the constant stream of small miracles announced by my sons. For them life was awesome and cardboard boxes were free. And so, thank goodness, were they.

They were free to do non-doing. Much of adult doing, from inner critiquing to our peer and familial interactions, are shaped by social pressures, both subtle and overt, that surround us. All our interactions are seen through these filters as if we see everything through tinted glasses. The filters provide a familiar explanation for the unfolding of the universe. Even our filters over time have filters. But children have no filters. The life they choose is the one they are living. Shunryu Suzuki called this naive sense of wonder "Zen Mind, Beginner's Mind," encouraging a childlike awe with everything we see, as if we are seeing it for the first time.

Wonder is an opening of the heart to the sublime majesty of this moment right here in front of us. It opens us to being wholly present to our life consisting as it does of "one continuous mistake," as Dogen wrote. Wonder arises in silence, where questions cease and answers aren't needed. It is either an awe-filled "Ah!" or an "Ah!"-filled awe. Wonder is many things, homonymic being just one of them.

55

On the way to Eungam Station in Seoul lived a tailor and his wife. He did simple alterations to pants and jackets. His wife did the measuring and the pinning. They had two large dry-cleaning machines, also her responsibility, as was the folding. He however did all the pressing. They both worked slowly. This being my favorite speed, I could relate. They took great care. They wore slippers because they lived upstairs. I always wanted a job in which I could wear slippers. Their home was part of the business and the business part of the home. They seemed very content.

I majored in philosophy. I discussed the big questions and pondered the small ones. Tying my shoelaces became an existential conundrum. My clothes, tattered and unwashed, reflected my state of mind. I dreamed of a life as a shepherd in Greece.

A good friend had not attended university. He started work right after high school and missed the entire 60s. He told me his ambition was to go into the dry-cleaning business. I stared at him, open-mouthed. What in the world was a dry cleaner? What was business? And what, pray tell, was ambition?

As I sat in the tailor's shop waiting in silence for my trousers to be tailored, I wondered if my old friend was not on to something. He should have argued his case with more vigor. He should have told me about the slippers.

Bare feet imply a surfer-dude approach to life in the stonerverse, filtering everything through a smoke of purple haze, confirming that the Dude still abides. Shoes, especially polished wing tips, indicate that above them stands a man of intent, sure of his gaze and the outcome of his days. But slippers? They say, "I take pride in my work, but I finish it on my terms, in my own style, and at my own speed."

56

I meditate mostly in my room, but I always meditate in silence. I remain still. Stillness is both a vehicle to silence and a byproduct of the same. Ajahn Chah referred to doing non-doing as a still forest pond. Stillness is also the antonym of distraction, whereas the conditioned mind is the epitome of distraction, filled as it is with well-trodden paths of judgment, impatience, craving, anger, and confusion. The myriad negative mind states prevent a banana from being seen as simply a banana. So pay attention but remain still. The metaphor most commonly used to combat distraction is to see all mind moments as clouds passing on a summer day. Even on a rainy day, behind the clouds the sky is blue, a deep azure as always. There is no need to chase the clouds away or bemoan that they are spoiling the day. They are just being clouds, taking care of cloud business. They will pass, and whether they do so quickly or otherwise, the sky remains still and silent.

Watching waves crashing on a rocky shore is a thrilling experience, but it blocks out subtler sounds and even overpowers more nuanced smells and tastes. It fills the mind. But the silence of a still forest pond empties the mind. It welcomes myriad other sounds, tastes, smells, and even thoughts to enter and rest a while. Stillness beckons the sounds of silence to join the non-doing mind in a concerto of emptiness, an ethereal hymnal that stretches to the heavens above.

A close cousin of silence, itself a result and a precursor to doing non-doing, is solitude. Solitude builds resilience and character to stand alone, a fearlessness at the gale-force winds imploring action and engagement. Heraclitus thought that "Various difficulties need not penetrate your soul but can remain external and non-affecting." Solitude is nothing to fear when you find comfort in a silent heart. Elephants walk, dogs bark.

Erling Kagge, author and explorer, the first man to solo walk to both poles, is an expert on both silence and solitude. He says both are invaluable. "You start to get answers to some questions you didn't know you had been asking yourself."

Solitude is not something to be feared, and it is not a synonym for loneliness. It is a state of mind and not necessarily a physical act. As the author Eleanor Catton wrote in her novel *The Luminaries*, "Solitude is a condition best enjoyed in company."

57

One parent-teacher evening, a parent caught me alone at my desk and asked to see me for a few minutes. She seemed upset over some perceived injustice or oversight. She started in on me before she had sat down.

"My Eliza in your grade 6 geography class received a failing grade on her last test. She had studied very hard for that test. She is very upset with the mark she got. How could you set such a difficult test? According to Eliza, you hadn't even taught half the material on the test."

Her barrage of accusations was so forceful that I thought to let her get it out of her system before I replied, so I said nothing. There were a few moments of awkward silence between us before she continued.

"Of course, when I say she studied hard I really don't know that for sure. Anyway, she spent a lot of time up in her room. She does have a television there and her own phone so maybe... How much time she actually spent buried in her books, I can't really say."

I said nothing.

"And I know she gets distracted in class and probably doesn't listen well. She's the same at home. Her mind is always elsewhere."

I said nothing.

"I can't imagine how you do it with children like Eliza. They don't pay attention, and they don't study. Yet they get upset when they don't do well on the tests, as if they are entitled to A's."

I said nothing.

"Anyway, I guess I just wanted to say how much I appreciate your effort with Eliza. That F you gave her has been a wake-up call. She is studying downstairs now where I can see her and help her if she asks. Thank you so much for all you've done for her." And with that, she shook my hand and walked out.

I had said nothing. In the past I have regretted many unkind and vexatious words that I have uttered, but I have never regretted my silence.

58

I don't do fun. I shun hysteria. I never understood the causal relationship between indulging in a fun activity and happiness. Having the bejesus scared out of me on a roller-coaster is not, in and of itself (as we used to insert into arguments in Philosophy 101), fun. It is terrifying. The fun can only arise, if at all, when the ride is over and you find yourself both back on terra firma, alive, and without having deposited your recently digested orange Slurpee all over your girlfriend. I chose simply to skip the terrifying stage and segue straight to the relief stage. I am not only happier for this, but I am $7.50 to the good. And my girlfriend is still talking to me.

I have concluded therefore that happy people, those truly content and at peace, do not need fun. There is no void in their life that requires filling. They are self-contained, like a three-colors-in-one pen. Many seek fun wherever and whenever, with ever-increasing levels of raucous jocularity, to keep the muddy morass of whatever lurks in their unconscious at a suitable distance. However, without a steady increase in the level of fun, in duration and intensity and its subsequent recording and posting on social media, the foreboding soundtrack of the grey abyss of despair can be heard just beyond the pale.

As the unconditioned beginner's mind is uncovered, peaks of pleasure lose their appeal. Like the Stoics of 2,000 years ago, a pleasant life was the goal, one best attained by a retired and simple approach. "Always look to what is inside," said the Stoics. Everything you need for happiness, joy, contentment, and peace reside there. Like the people looking at shadows on the wall from the fire in Plato's cave who took these zephyrs to be real and therefore produced a form of happiness and status by guessing what will arrive next on the wall, outside of us reside only shadows of happiness, joy, contentment, and peace—zephyrs of delusion, usurping our attention from all that is truly worthy.

59

I have spent most of my adult life avoiding gainful employment. I remember telling my guidance counselor at the age of fourteen that I wanted to be a shepherd. I pictured myself lazing under a giant oak, my trusty staff at my side, ready to rescue any wayward sheep. But shepherding was not on his list of future occupations, so he checked off actuary for me. For years I thought the two were synonymous. I once met a man who worked at an insurance office. He said he was an actuary. I was thrilled. I asked him where his staff was. "Why, at the office, of course," he replied.

I put shepherding out of my mind for many years after that. I did, however, stay on the lookout for jobs with a shepherdian level of activity. A job that followed the KISS rule: Keep It Simple, Stupid. And I found such a job in Seoul. It was a key-making shop built on the sidewall of a garage. It was just wide enough for the owner to sit in his chair. From there he could reach every key in his store. The store itself was all glass. The front door was of the sliding variety and made of glass, but you couldn't use it. You couldn't actually enter the shop. You stopped at the threshold and passed the key to be duplicated to the owner. The owner never left his chair. He would make the duplicate and pass it back to you. He took your money and placed it in an old cigar box. There was no room for a cash register.

I think I would like to work in such a store. You can see your entire inventory. When you don't have any keys to duplicate, you can look through the glass walls and door at the people passing by. You can make yourself a cup of tea and relax. You don't need to sweep up in your free time. You don't need to worry about shoplifting. There is no need for a security camera, because no one actually comes into your store. When someone stands at your door you can be pretty sure what they want. You're not going to be stumped by a tricky question. I think I'd like all that. It's not as good as being a shepherd, but if you have to live in a city it's a good job. Besides, your keys don't wander away and get caught on a cliff, so you don't need a big staff.

60

As one proceeds on the non-doing path, the simpler life becomes. The simplicity refers to a lessening of inner confusion, not necessarily to fewer possessions. A letting go or a discarding happens naturally to all the habitual mind patterns that we immerse ourselves in. Again, it's the craving for and our attachment to our chosen modes of escape that subside. With increased insight into how our attachments create more misery than relief, they may indeed fall off our radar. But it is just as likely that all that drops are our conditioned responses, and with newfound clarity we make a conscious choice to continue an old habit. After all, we remain human beings, and we continue to do the stuff of human beings, which today might include speculating about moving or about what car, if any, we should buy, etc. Doing non-doing does not negate taking responsibility for our family, our friends, and ourselves so as not to be a burden to others.

I had a friend in a rock group who began to meditate. He quit the group, thinking music was not conducive to progress on the path. He was right, but he was also miserable. In time, he re-affirmed his love of music without all the mind games and drug problems associated with it. Leonard Cohen spent a good part of his life living and practicing meditation on Mount Baldy in California, where he composed some of his best songs. Simplicity entails less attachment and craving. It need not include abandonment. You are not under duress to renounce comfort and luxury. While the teachings may frown upon the race to the top, they also do not condone a race to the bottom.

Sayagyi U Ba Khin was a much-revered meditation master in Burma. He was also a family man with a wife and children.

As well, he was the Accountant General in the government. He was so famous for his honesty and distaste for the practice of bribery that the president asked him to take on the responsibility of two other government departments simultaneously. In the evenings he would attend to his students at his meditation center. By all outward appearances this was a busy man. In truth he simply did all that was asked of him with an unbusy mind. The more unbusy his mind, the more jobs he could take on.

My first teacher was Roshi Philip Kapleau, the first American to become a Zen monk. After hearing a lecture by D.T. Suzuki, he gave everything he had away and went to Japan to ordain. For him the path was clear. For Sayagyi, who was immersed in the Dhamma since birth, there was little to romanticize in taking robes; monks were as common on the streets of Yangon as pigeons in New York. Sayagyi continued to work hard for the rest of his life, living as if his life in government service was real. The Dhamma may be our foundation, it may guide all our actions and thoughts, but we need not turn it into a lifestyle to prove the depth of our commitment.

61

When I was young, we were a family of four living in a small apartment. At the time, especially as a teenager, I bemoaned my lot in life and wished I lived in a far grander home like a few of my friends.

My mother fancied herself a philosopher. She read Lin Yutang and Richard Needham of the Toronto Globe and Mail. My father was an army guy, a vet who lived for hockey and football. My mother had no one with whom she could discuss the issues of the day until I came along. Newspaper in hand, she would come at me as I was getting dressed to go out and play and begin by saying, "This is quite interesting…" Then she would read to me the entire editorial, following me from room to room. But persistence alone couldn't explain her ability to get through to me. You might say that my whole academic life changed for the better, at least in part, because of the smallness of our apartment. I was a fast kid and could deke with the best of them, but there was no place to fake left, go right in such a small apartment. If she thought I might make a dash for it, she would position herself like a middle linebacker in front of the door (we only had one) and simply read louder. Eventually, I realized there was no escape. I had no choice but to listen. It didn't take too long before I started to enjoy hearing about different points of view. She was a hippie before the term came into vogue, planting the idea that there was more to life than amassing lots of stuff and getting a well-paying job. She was very happy much later when I majored in philosophy.

While we weren't poor, we were not profligate by any means, being staunch Scottish Protestants and all. Our little apartment had few furnishings, but those we had were good quality and lasted the twenty years I lived there. Frugality ruled the roost, though. And the fact that four of us lived in this small sanctuary to domestic downsizing meant that everything had its place, and heaven help the miscreant who forgot to return something to its appointed home or left their homework on the dining table.

Later in life it was very easy for me to slip into a simple Zen environment, because that was the way I was raised. And today I still wear the same cloak of frugality, much to the consternation of my own children. I eventually saw the wisdom of the old axiom, "Unhappy is the man with many keys," or at least its superiority compared to its profligate antithesis.

I recall only once as a child crying for my parents to buy me something. I wanted a toy cement mixer I had seen at a shoe store where we were shopping. I kicked up quite a fuss and eventually my mother relented.

I rushed home and went to the local sandbox with my new toy. I showed it to all my friends. We would spend hours every day building huge forts, and now I could be the alpha male because I had the only cement mixer. Except, of course, the cement mixer didn't actually mix cement or anything for that matter. I soon tired of it. However, I learned two things that day. Firstly, if I cried long enough and loud enough, my parents would buy me almost anything I wanted. This was sort of comforting, except for the second thing I learned. Having a meltdown to get something was not a pleasant feeling. I felt badly that I had essentially blackmailed my parents, and I swore I would never do that again. And I never did.

62

Because we aren't trying to get better or happier or stronger or wealthier, our life advice no longer needs to come from style gurus and lifestyle coaches. (What is a lifestyle anyway? And why does it need coaching?) Of course, we aren't trying to get sadder or weaker or poorer either. We are simply living a more unconditioned life, a more honest life, more content with our lot. We have not exchanged one overtly conditioned mindset for another, seemingly cooler, conditioned mindset. It is easy to fall into the trap of abandoning all the trappings of your conventional life only to take on all the trappings of your new "meditative" lifestyle.

Stay awake, especially if you become aware that you talk only of all the retreats you have been on, are soon to go on, or hope to go on sometime in the future. Stay awake. Is there a hierarchy in the group? All groups have a hierarchy, so the answer is simply, "yes." More importantly, do you envy those above you? Do you hate them? Do you indulge in all the latest vegetarian food fads? Have you and others developed a unique group speech pattern? Do you have any friends outside of your fellow meditators? And after many years of practice, are you now in a senior position of authority with similar trappings of status and power to your job at IBM? The work is to stay awake to all the habit patterns of the mind. Envy, status, and group think do not get relegated to the remainder bin because you exchanged a three-piece suit for maroon robes. Simplicity is a state of mind, not a display of ascetism.

At one time I was a senior assistant teacher in a Burmese meditation tradition. I thought myself unattached to my status. If we teachers had a Mr. America Contest, I would have won the Most Humble trophy. When I started a family,

I surrendered my duties and responsibilities thereby placing myself out of the loop. A full teacher in that tradition observed my underlying angry reaction to certain supposed actions of a few of my old comrades. He was quite right, and I thank him even today for that wake-up call. I didn't realize how much I was attached to the key to the executive suite bathroom. I enjoyed being on the inside track and now, on the outside peering through the foggy windows of power, I imagined conspiracies and underhandedness. Yes, I had resigned my position, but I had forgotten to turn in my attachment to my status. Not to mention, my trophy.

We are freeing ourselves of old habits, and in so doing we are free to see that the life we have is perfect just as it is. This is why one of the symbols of the path has always been the lotus flower. This beautiful flower grows in the muddy swamps of South and Southeast Asia. Similarly, every life can be the source of a beautiful arising despite the bog you are living in. "Your heart is always whole, just as the moon is always full. Your life is always complete," according to Karen Maezen Miller.

63

I like to bake bread. Actually, the bread bakes itself; I simply facilitate the process. I add the flour to the yeast and water. I then knead the mixture, but even in this most tactile of experiences I am more an engaged observer than a creator. Kneading continues until the mixture reveals to my hands and fingers that the mixture is well kneaded. I do not know how long this takes, nor can I tell a would-be baker what it should feel like when it is done. The dough and I work together, altering the strength and speed of the kneading as we see fit. The whole process unfolds in a pasdedough of divine dimensions. I am not trying to improve, but I am getting better at it. No one is teaching me, but I am learning.

The dough is left to rise. It does so whether I watch it or not. Again, I do nothing except see to it that no impediments to the rising are present. The bread trusts me to do my part, and I allow it to do its part. Lao Tzu might say I am doughing non-doughing.

64

When someone says hello to me in Korean, I invariably reply "kamsahamnida." My response is immediate and trips naturally off my tongue. Unfortunately "kamsahamnida" does not mean "hello." It means, "thank you." But I don't care. To my ear, "kamsahamnida" sounds like a greeting. It sounds more like a greeting than the proper greeting, "annyeonghaseyo," which gets caught in my throat like a mouthful of Brillo. The interesting thing is that the Koreans to whom I reply seem to accept my thank you as a kind of greeting. Koreans don't often say thank you. Maybe they have forgotten what it means. True, I bow and smile when I say it. I turn it into a greeting. Maybe they are not paying close attention. But I think they tune into my intention, and intention, they say, is the better part of valor. Actually it's discretion that is the better part of valor. But surely intention is the better part of some aphorism and so explains how I get away with saying one thing when I mean to say another.

My greeting experience has led me to rethink the basic rules of language acquisition and second language communication. I have thrown the rule book away. I rely on intention. I say what I want to say in my heart and open my mouth, and whatever comes out will be understood by one and all, because my intention was clear, right word be damned! Sometimes I don't even have the wrong word in mind. Or I may have the right word, but it is in Hindi or Burmese. Again, I fall back on my intention. I smile, I gesture, I shrug my shoulders, I hand over a wad of won, I trust, and all of a sudden, I am given a ticket and the door opens. You don't need language when your intention is pure. I have transcended language. I have gone beyond the mundane rules of grammar and syntax.

I am reborn. I am Minerva, god of communication. The world is my home, and intention is my language. Searching for the proper word is just so linguistically constipating.

65

From my small hut atop a hill in Maharashtra, I could watch the farmers on the plains below. Late afternoon was my favorite time of day. The cow dust hour, it was called, and for good reason. The cows kicked up reddish dust as they were herded home from the pastures. The farmers sang to them as they moved them along to dinner and milking. This scene had been played out since time long forgotten. It reflected a natural rhythm to life. An unhurried purpose presided over each day. Cows needed to eat every day. They needed to be milked every day. They left little room in the pastures for anxiety to graze. I doubt the farmer thought of happiness or fulfillment or even tomorrow, for that matter. The Stoics talked of a life in tune with nature, and here before my eyes was a living example of just such a life. Perhaps a cow herder in Maharashtra is not your cup of tea. You wish to remain an insurance salesman in Omaha. Fine and good. But ask yourself—at the end of your busy day on the commute home, do you sing?

66

To be a Buddhist is to be a Stoic and to be a Stoic is to be a Buddhist. Neither is a religion. Mere belief in their precepts holds no purchase. Reciting them every morning proves futile. Both speak of universal truths and natural laws that govern human and social behavior. Both schools are empirical, which is to say they are evidence-based. And that itself is grounded or tested, even, on one's own experience. They both conclude that happiness lies within and that it is compromised by our aberrant thoughts and that these irrational, harmful, delusional, obsessive, and fanciful meanderings must be ignored or, better, understood, before taking any action. The Stoics arrived at their position through philosophical investigation of a man with a mind; the Buddha found enlightenment through self-reflection and analysis of the mind within a man.

The basis for the management of human frailty is morality. The Stoics refrained from antisocial behavior, irritability, excess passion, dishonesty, and thoughtlessness. The five Buddhist principles consist of refraining from taking life, taking what has not been freely given, abstaining from sexual misconduct, improper speech, and intoxicants. Both base their guidelines on personal experience. You will find yourself happier or calmer when you behave more in tune with nature.

When we ignore the laws of nature out of ignorance and act only in our own self-interest, even if we gain the whole world, we are bound to be unhappy. And there is no excuse or justification for wallowing in self-pity or past grievances which perpetuate unmindful, even vengeful, actions. We are all free to act with reason and compassion no matter how we might have been tormented or suppressed. Sharon Salzberg proclaims adamantly that "We are not stuck in any way." We can be better, we can rise above, we do not need to dwell in remorse and spite. We can love, we can smile, and we can wail.

Everyone's life shuttlecocks between gain and loss, honor and dishonor, praise and blame, happiness and unhappiness. Such yin and yang come to all of us in lesser or greater amounts; no one is exempt. Don't try to be someone you aren't. And don't hide, for there is nothing weird or wrong with you. Let the extroverts, the opiners, the trendies, the cool guys and gals, the alphas, the Twitterverse have their day; it won't be a long or very sunny one. As Graydon Carter says, "Celebrities have the shelf life of milk." And 2,000 years before that, Marcus Aurelius asked, "How is it that every man has more love of himself than all the rest of the world but yet sets less value on his own opinion of himself than on the opinion of others?"

You may not be the funniest or the most popular or the most charismatic. But you are the only you. And if you can just be you, free of the conditioning to be everyone else's idea of the perfect you, your grace, kindness, and honesty will eventually win the day. To quote the character Lester Bangs from the movie "Almost Famous": "The only true currency in this bankrupt world is what you share with someone else when you're not cool."

67

I was too thin to have good quality clothes fit me well. When I wore a suit, my head looked too small. When I turned my head while wearing a collar and tie, neither collar nor tie moved. Like a compass, my tie always pointed north. If it weren't for the sleeves, I could perform a full 360-degree rotation without my suit getting a wrinkle. But in the end, this proved a real blessing.

My misalignment meant I could buy all my clothes at thrift stores. Well-washed shirts and pants fit loosely. I wasn't thin; my clothes were simply older and had lost their shape. Secondly, my lack of sartorial splendor freed me to think of other matters besides looking good for the opposite sex. Thirdly, I could be funny. If you look very svelte and cool in an Armani suit, referred to as the full Clooney, you can't put onion dip up your nose and expect a laugh.

Be yourself. See the silliness of trying to be someone else's idea of you. It's exhausting keeping up a front. Don't behave, live. Be yourself. You might as well, as George Burns said, because everyone else is already taken.

And it is not only Hollywood comedians who feel this way. Polonius advised his son, Laertes, "To thine own self be true," as I'm sure we all would agree. But the idea begs the question, to which self should I be true? Certainly not the conditioned self, that amalgam of habits and pressures and posturing. Doing non-doing exposes these faux personas, and they do calm enough over time so that you may abide the desire to jump at every opportunity to reinforce your reputation.

Suppose you aspire to be someone special to escape your earlier life situations. Perhaps you were poor, had no friends, or were bullied. Your early years were a misery, and you lacked the skillful means to simply see it as such. You might naturally have sought solace in your dreams, perhaps of being a rock star. Let us assume for the sake of the argument that you succeeded. You are now rich, with lots of friends, and now you can be the bully. You made it! Except now you suffer from rock star conditions. These are certainly different from the poor conditions you escaped, but better? Your status now remains only as high as the sales of your last album or last tour. Your friends are mostly hangers-on. You must continue to generate millions of dollars a year just to keep your head above water. You have probably developed a nasty drug habit to deal with all the pressure. And of course, you are one incriminating video short of having the whole deck of cards come crashing down on your profligate little head.

The particulars of your conditioned mind have changed, but the essence remains the same. You continue to react habitually to all these conditions of mind either with craving or aversion or confusion. Your life, before and after living your dream, remains one big mistake, differing only in the details. Once you achieve your dream, you are no longer dreaming. You are, just like the rest of us, living a life. *Plus la change, plus la meme chose.*

68

On my way to school one bitterly cold winter's day, I passed a house in the early stages of being built. The workers were framing the roof. The wind was howling, the snow was blowing, and they kept at it because that is what we all must do. We choose our path...roofer, physicist, or, like me, a solo contemplative on a hilltop in India. But we hone our craft every day, even on those days we don't want to work.

No matter the path, the mind is similar. It gets bored, it gets tired of the familiar, and it craves escape when the going gets tough. This is the constant. Changing jobs or locations or responsibilities will not alter our habitual mindset to seek a more pleasant pursuit and hate whatever we find unpleasant and to bounce back and forth between the two, without any understanding of how to transcend the human condition.

Our responsibilities, our work, our service to others, our companionship, is human work. It's what makes us *sapiens.* It matters not a jot if this work plays out on the world stage or in a hut on a hill in India. You get up each day and do it again, to quote the singer and poet Jackson Brown. Another poet, Robert Frost, wrote:

The woods are lovely, dark, and deep,
But I have promises to keep,
And miles to go before I sleep,
And miles to go before I sleep.

69

The more I investigate and dissect what I focus my attention on with clear comprehension, the more apparent becomes the changing nature of the mind and body. I don't have to chase away any uncomfortable feelings or pains with alcohol or drugs or various distractions. I am less inclined to succumb to their whispered promise to stop being the person I am for this one evening and become someone better. If I do nothing, these temptations will be seen as the lies they are, and they will calm. Unfortunately for the more pleasant mind states and bodily feelings, the same law of impermanence applies. We can't control this flux. Back aches may get worse, and love diminishes. *C'est la vie.*

We suffer because we identify with this pain. It is my back ache after all. My best friend doesn't suffer any pain from my back ache. As we dissect everything in the mind and in the body, it becomes clear that I suffer from my back ache because I have a body and I suffer from my divorce because I have a mind which craves what I once had. And I have a body and a mind because I was born.

This is not a trite discovery. It is very profound. If you have a body, you will suffer aches, pains, illness, old age, and eventually death. If you have a mind, you will suffer from greed, hatred, and delusion. None of this is your fault. Pain is going on 24/7, and there is not a thing you can do about it. Why is this? For the simple reason that there is no "you" to do something about the suffering. There is no soul, no unified self, experiencing the pain.

We can experience this insubstantiality when we meditate. I dissect pain and emotion, blockages and mind states, and as I do so, their ephemeral nature becomes clear. The suffering diminishes when I stay out of it, when I keep the pain as sensations in the body, when I keep the sadness as a feeling in the mind. I don't identify with what is going on. Ajahn Katiko tells us, "There is nothing to fear because there is no condition that is a problem. Neither the condition nor the fear is us." Owning the suffering or the joy perpetuates the myth of the ego or the soul. I am not the center of the universe. I am not even the center of the body/mind. "I" am not.

Take a car, for example. A car is a concept. There is the body on which are many parts, the wheels, the seats, the door handles, etc. that help the car to function. Take those off and set them aside. And there is a running system, the so-called brain that makes the car go. This includes the computer that watches over the whole operation as well as the electrical connections, the engine, the exhaust system, etc. Take them off as well and set them aside. What is left? Nothing. Where is the car? It's nowhere to be found. "Car" is simply a word we use to refer to the sum of all the parts. Behind the parts there is no entity, no unifying carness, no car essence. And it is the same with you and me.

70

Bhante Rahula and I would meditate outside on some very flat but hard boulders because that summer was particularly hot. On this particular day, I crossed my legs and straightened my spine as usual. I closed my eyes, and almost immediately I felt nothing but subtle vibrating throughout my entire being. It appeared I had dissolved into pulsations. I felt no solidity. I had become a hologram. I opened my eyes just once to check. And yes, I was still there. Relieved that at least my legs where still where I had left them, I closed my eyes and continued the meditation.

I tried to move my attention through my body, but this proved quite difficult without a solid body and all. So I just paid attention to the vibrations. Except I couldn't tell where "my" vibrations ended and the boulder's began. This made some sense, since I figured the boulder had been meditating there for about 10,000 years. I managed to keep my attention somewhat within my corporeal structure, concerned as I was of floating off into space and disrupting the space/time continuum.

The seated meditation ended, and we returned to the dining *sala* for tea. I walked back as usual. One foot after the other. No big thing, really except for my whole being melting away. Everything was the same, but everything was different. There really was no one home, no unified self. Just a pile of vibrations like everything else in the universe.

Do I feel this subtle pulsating all the time now? Of course not. I have two teenage sons! But I know the pulsating is there, and sometimes that is enough.

71

The summer after high school, Tony, his younger brother Chris, and I set out in an old Vauxhall held together with spit and bailing wire for points west on the Trans-Canada Highway. We camped the entire way and cooked over an open fire. Once we reached the Pacific, we headed south to the Oregon hills before turning east and eventually home and university. On the way we camped near Mount Rushmore, hoping to see the famous presidential sculptures the next morning.

The next morning broke rainy and cold. Our tent flooded, and an open fire was impossible. Looking like drowned rats, we drove to the only restaurant around, in the luxurious hotel in front of the mountain. The restaurant served a formal breakfast, its patrons dressed well. We, on the other hand, hadn't seen a tablecloth in five weeks. Its floor-to-ceiling window looked out on the famous sculpture. We hesitated at the main entrance, thinking our drenched, odorous, and disheveled selves not worthy of such a fine dining experience.

A very young maître d' greeted us and asked if we wanted a table. We said no and that we could only afford toast and coffee. He said for that, we still needed a table. We said we hadn't dressed, and furthermore we weren't guests at the hotel. We were camping, and we were flooded out.

Without missing a beat, he asked us to follow him. As we walked, every eye in the dining room was on us. He led us to a table right at the window with a perfect (and very dry) view of the presidents. A waiter appeared. The maître d' informed him that we were friends of his, and we would be having only toast and coffee. The waiter departed with our order, and our friend the maître d' returned to his station.

Whatever kindnesses I have shown to others over my life, of which there have been far too few to mention and none to rave about, were birthed in that restaurant on that cold and rainy day. A young man not much older than I, probably a university student working as a summer intern, decided to do the kind thing. It was for him, as it always is, a choice to be made. It is made from the heart, which for whatever inexplicable reason, had at that time opened. And when it does, it is important to act quickly before the conditioned mind can intervene with reasonable objections or fears of possible tragic consequences. Never disregard a plea from the heart to simply do the kind thing.

Every act of kindness is like a pebble thrown into a still pond. The ripples emanate for a long time afterwards, striking the shoreline at different places and at different times, sometimes long after the initial act of throwing the stone. And so it is with kindness. Kindness begets kindness. A smile is almost always returned and usually passed on and on. This is the ripple effect. The kindness of that young maître d' has been rippling on for almost fifty years now. So perhaps this little book is just me inviting you to breakfast at the best seat in the house, offering a view of a mountain that may change your life.

72

I think there is a place in our lives for tradition and even ritual. They keep our lives simple and understandable. In our family we have pancakes every Sunday and tea every evening. We go for walks together. We spend a month every summer at our cottage. We watch a movie every Friday night.

I don't like variety, and I'm not fond of change. Holidays disrupt my daily routine and cancel my daily newspaper. I am a creature of habits, but for a very good reason. I like my routines. That's how they became routines in the first place. I wanted to do them day after day. If I did not like my rituals, I would not do them. Why would I eat toast for breakfast rather than porridge if I really wanted to eat porridge? Would I eat toast just to be adventurous? To push the envelope? To live on the edge? If I wanted adventure, I'd swim the Amazon. I'm not going to switch breakfast cereals and write a book about my experience. The trouble is, I don't like adventure either. For a writer this presents a challenge. I don't have a lot I can write about. And as I said, I'm not going to swim the Amazon. Anyway, I'm sure the porridge there would be soggy.

The unconditioned mind is a free mind, emancipated from the incarceration of old habit patterns that sought answers, pleasures, fun, and status in the ten thousand things found under the bright lights. It is free to live a simpler life where previously mundane tasks take on a glow in their familiar embrace of the joy of simple things. Every day, every moment for that matter, bears a familiarity to every other day and every moment. Like snowflakes, however, each is unique in its own way. Every day, every moment can be experienced for the first time. You see daily life as a very young child, immersed in wonder and joy at the unfolding of life itself. Today was the first time I ate the porridge I made this morning.

Neuronally constructed habit patterns predispose us to obsessive behaviors, addictions, and a psychological anomaly referred to as cognitive dissonance. The latter is defined in Webster's as "anxiety that results from simultaneously holding contradictory or otherwise incompatible attitudes, beliefs or the like." In more simple terms, cognitive dissonance is behind the old joke, "My mind is made up. Don't confuse me with the facts." And these habit patterns have serious implications in social and political discourse. Our psychology is already predisposed to believing things that are comforting and peer-reaffirming rather than true.

Fake news that supports a certain world view is more likely to be cited and passed on than true facts that question or contradict one's view. Because of the persistent deepening and reinforcement of neurotransmitters, our biases have become deeply ingrained and less likely to be overridden by statistics or facts to the contrary. Op-ed pages may be wonderfully written and researched, but they are singing to the choir, boring to those who agree with the pundits and ignored by those who are opposed.

73

I loved to go fishing with my father, because he was a terrible fisherman. He never caught anything. I was fine with this. I didn't like to put a worm on the hook. I didn't like taking the hook out of the fish's mouth, and I certainly couldn't bash the head of the fish against the seat of the boat to kill it.

In the summer at our cottage, my father went fishing every morning and evening. It was always very quiet, the water as still as the night sky. My father would disturb the silence only to suggest we try "over there," knowing fully well that "over there" wouldn't produce any more action than right here. Nevertheless, he would steer the punt to a shoal or a shallow bay with a surety, as if some fisher oracle had bequeathed the secret teachings just moments after we left our dock.

Sometimes we'd troll, sometimes we'd cast. Dad would change lures every fifteen minutes or so. I, on the other hand, didn't want to change the luck. I had chosen the one lure that seemed the least likely to be swallowed by any self-respecting fish. I was content to just sit and let the waves take us wherever they wished. I so enjoyed my time on the lake that after a while I left the lure in the box. I just dropped a line over the side and let the weights keep it below the surface. I think my father knew I wasn't actually fishing. I like to think he didn't say anything because he enjoyed the company. I think he liked to hang out with someone who liked the quiet and the peace as much as he did.

He was a terrible fisherman. He never caught anything. Yet year after year he would use the same lures that had shown themselves to be complete duds. I still go to the same cottage with my family. I take a kayak out and paddle to the middle of the lake and drift back to shore. Then I paddle back out and repeat. I call it paddling non-paddling. If my father is watching me, I am sure he would relate to the peace and quiet-drifting part, but he would question my lack of fishing tackle. What will people think?

The silent mind is more likely to welcome a silent natural environment. When I am out on the lake, my silence welcomes the call of the loon, which in no way interrupts the silence or disturbs me in any way. His plaintive call is such a part of the lake, it is as if the lake, the kayak, and the loon and I are floating on the silence. Silence both within as a welcomed state of mind and without as a reflection of the natural state of the unconditioned mind can be seen as the antidote to the daily conundrums of life. A confused mind often seeks out noise in the form of music, conversation, debates, and sermons to negate the fear of silence. Silence is seen as death as opposed to what it really is, namely a wellspring for ideas. Non-doing thrives in silence. Remaining awake, alert, and watchful is the gateway to being truly alive.

A walk in the woods takes on another dimension when undertaken in silence. In Japan shinrin-yoku, or forest bathing, is a part of a natural healing process. People eat less and remain more mindful when they eat in silence. Arguments made for or against something are softer and less conflicting when they come from silence. When confronted by a purposefully impossible-to-answer question posited by a wise pundit to embarrass him, the Buddha would remain silent. Christians have long associated silence with all that is holy. "Silent Night. Holy Night," in which all is calm and all is bright. T.S. Eliot sounded as much like a Buddhist as a Christian when he said, "If we really want to pray, we must first learn to listen, for in the silence of the heart God speaks."

74

I loved the water buffalo I encountered in India. Despite their girth and their horns, they were very gentle creatures. They calmly abided all and sundry afflictions, heat, mosquitoes, and monsoon rains without so much as a by-your-leave. Other than whisking away unwanted bitey things with their tails, they endured, and they did so ever so calmly.

The buffs were an inspiration to me when I lived in South Asia. I was an educated, relatively wealthy Westerner when I first went to India. That is to say, I was miserable. The heat, the dust, the filth, and the monsoons were overpowering. But over time watching the buffaloes, I came to understand that I was being buffeted by the same conditions that the uneducated and woefully underpaid buffaloes calmly abided. When I asked myself who the wiser of two was, the answer was obvious, and it sure wasn't the one with three university degrees.

From then on when my practice would wane, I took on my water buffalo anima. I relaxed my face muscles, unhunched my shoulders, and just sat there, tethered to my cushion. "Water buffalo mind," I called it. I've had many teachers over the years, but the water buffalo were the only ones who taught in silence. Thankfully, they were also the only ones with horns.

75

Years ago, when I would walk around my house late at night after everyone else was asleep, it felt like I had always lived there. I liked that it felt that way. As my oldest son said when he was three, "It feels as perfect as right." I knew where the hardwood floors creaked, and I avoided those spots so I wouldn't wake the baby who, like me, was a light sleeper. My wife and my five-year-old, he of the aphorism above, slept the sleep of the dead. I could drop a refrigerator on the creaky spots and they wouldn't stir.

I think it's important to know where the creaky spots are. Sometimes convention demands that you avoid them. At other times, maybe when you're alone or you just want to push the envelope, it's comforting to hear a familiar creak. Late at night, it's kind of reassuring that you're in the right house.

In hindsight I realize life is a quest. Some look for riches, others for fame. I look for reassurance. As a child I would lie in bed in my room, and every so often I would call out, "Daddy?" He would grunt or throw a slipper at me, but whatever, it was good to know he hadn't stolen away in the middle of the night. As an older teen I tried talking to God, but he must have been elsewhere. So, for me, it's floor creaks.

So there I stand, even today at the witching hour. The familiar sounds of my two sons' breathing in their rooms, my wife's soft snoring in ours, and my walking back and forth across the creaky spots. My wife hears me and asks me what I'm doing. "Talking to God," I tell her. "I'm still on hold."

We all have our own Garden of our Familiar. The more Familiars I have, and doing non-doing has allowed many such gardens to appear, the less I crave the hip, the cool, and the latest.

I don't know if this puts me behind the curve or ahead of the curve. For instance, I have never owned a smartphone. People thought I was stupid. Now everyone is worried that smartphones are making them lonely and miserable. They're being banned in schools. Some pundits now think I was on the right track to never own one. And I left Facebook many years ago, fed up with getting special notices every time some "friend" changed their cat's picture. Now people are doing the same thing, concerned their private data was compromised. I don't understand what the problem is. Why do the Russians care that I eat oatmeal? Why is the entire Twitterverse apparently concerned about my breakfast peccadilloes. Bob Dylan made a similar point when he advised us to not follow leaders and watch for parking meters. The idea has more of a ring of truth when the rhyme is good.

~ 76

In Korea it is considered rude to speak immediately after someone else has just spoken. Korean culture demands a slight pause to indicate the listeners have fully digested and appreciated the input. It gives them pause for thought. This promotes civilized dialogue in which everyone's view is respected. It also calms blind reactions to some perceived fault in the argument. A pause is a conscious decision to take a breath and become aware of physical sensations like heartbeat, dry mouth, etc. that may indicate the would-be speaker is already strongly reacting to what was said and so might choose his next words carefully. It is the pause that refreshes.

When delivering a controversial suggestion to a colleague, a pause can tune you in to conflicting undercurrents of social pressures, biases, hyperbole, prejudice, and political correctness that have subconsciously influenced your proposition. A pause clears the mind of such ulterior issues, enabling you to speak more truthfully. A pause deposits your old baggage in the trunk of the car momentarily. Then it is up to you whether or not you want to drive your stuff to the Goodwill store.

77

Doing non-doing deconditions the mind so that a happy life, defined by the Stoics as true, virtuous, and natural, arises like a phoenix from the ashes of the conditioned mind. Since the real shift is within you, your new life may retain all the appearances of your old life. After all, the difference, they say, between heaven and hell is a mere sixteenth of an inch, surely an imperceptible amount of change in the grand scheme of things.

In my case that shift was substantial, though I arrived there incrementally. My new life fit me like an old glove but required quite a leap of faith for friends and family. They had been quite happy with me living a lie. But the new me seemed happy, and I wasn't hurting anyone, so I was finally given a pass. And as I was single and modestly moneyed, I set out to see where my "don't know mind" might take me. I was somewhat inspired by Walt Whitman, for whom the loafer was venerated, belonging as he did "to that ancient and honorable fraternity, whom I venerate above all your upstarts, your dandies, and your political oracles." That was me in a nutshell. I did not, however, think of myself as a loafer.

And so, after a lifetime of idle wandering punctuated by modestly productive cafe sitting and extended periods of meditation pursuing non-doing, imagine my surprise when I discovered at my advanced age that my aforementioned vagabond life had a designated title: flaneur. Trust the French to come up with a proper, almost professional title for a life of mindful breathing.

Oui. Je suis un flaneur: an idler, an observer of minutia, a noticer. And at times a writer and teacher of the same. That hits the nail on the head. I have at long last a job title, and an exotic one at that, one with panache. I feel like I should order some business cards. Ian McCrorie…Professional Flaneur. It sure beats reprobate. The money is the same, but flaneur just sounds so much more financially endowed.

Who else but the French, the inventors of the cafe, could come up with a proper name for their patrons? Without the cafe, Hemingway would have remained a hack journalist. He was the quintessential flaneur, and it was his flaneuricity that eventually produced "The Sun Also Rises." To flaneur, if it could be verbed, is to meditate with coffee and notepad.

And to think, my friends used to call me a slug. No more. Je suis un flaneur. Now they'll have to *manger their mots*.

78

One summer I drove a truck for an oil company. Two of us installed the oil tanks for furnaces in the basement of houses. It was dirty work. The basements were often unheated. They were seldom clean. One day, it was particularly cold and rainy. We entered through the back door into the kitchen. On my way to the basement stairs I came upon the owners, two unwed older sisters having a breakfast of tea and toast. The tea had just been poured, and the toast, freshly buttered, awaited the jam. The oven was on, its door open to take the chill off. How I wished my cold, wet self could pull up a chair and join them.

This was an epiphany for me. It struck me that on a cold and rainy day, having tea and toast in a cozy kitchen with your family was the ultimate happiness. Because the sisters were having a new furnace installed, a great inconvenience compounded by the weather conditions, they had no choice but to spend the next few hours drinking tea and eating toast. If I was right that this was really, on that particular morning, the ultimate happiness, then surely it was available to everyone. And if so, what is the point of running around like chickens with their heads cut off chasing the almighty dollar? Tea, toast, friends, and a warm kitchen. Enough.

The happiest countries in surveys invariably are those in Scandinavia. Norwegians speak of *koselig*, inspired by the Danish *hygge*, one of their many words for happiness, roughly translated as sitting around with family. They also employ the word *peiskos* which literally means to sit in front of a crackling fireplace and enjoy the heat. Another synonym for happiness in Norway is *kukelfure*, which is to sit and think about things while doing nothing at all. (I take exception to this definition, of course, in that thinking about things is not doing nothing.)

In Iceland the word *solarfri* is used when workers are given unexpected time off to enjoy a sunny day. The Swedish word *gökotta* literally means to wake up early to hear the first bird sing. I personally think Tagalog comes closest to the mark with the word *gigil,* which is the irresistible urge to pinch someone because they are loved.

The tea and toast epiphany stayed with me as an ideal, but it was only as I practiced non-doing and the conditioned mind quieted enough that I could really live it. Like David Copperfield, who wondered if he would become the hero of his own life, doing non-doing wrestles control of your future away from the conditioning agents that have you programmed to react and behave and even think as they want. We can be the hero of our own life or remain the servant of our own ingrained habit patterns.

Remember the words of W.E. Henley from his poem "Invictus,"

It matters not how strait the gate,
How charged with punishments the scroll,
I am the master of my fate,
I am the captain of my soul.

79

Our cottage is on a small lake on the Canadian Shield. Our shoreline is very rocky, with large boulders deposited there as the glaciers retreated 10,000 years ago. Amazingly this shoreline provides sufficient sustenance for trees to grow and, in their own way, thrive. They protrude out perpendicularly from crevices between the rocks before turning upwards to catch a modicum of sunlight and spread their gnarly majesty.

These trees are my Dhamma teachers, encapsulating the entire teachings. Some trees never grew, unable to maintain a foothold in the rocky outcropping. Others grew for a few years but remained stunted and shriveled due to a lack of sunshine. And some established a plethora of roots and soared to a good height. Even a few made it to a normal height, but in the end this made little difference, for these alpha trees were cut down to provide a view for the cottagers.

This is life. We all have a limited time. Some die before they are born while others are with us well into their nineties. Some are healthy right to the very end; others suffer a variety of ailments their entire life. This is just the way it is. Everything and everyone is born, stays a while, and dies. Our mental states, our emotions, our anger, our worry, and all our physical aches and pains, when left to their own devices, with understanding also take birth, stay a while, and eventually pass on. They linger longer only when we hurry them along or try to sweep them under the carpet.

80

Matthew 21:22 promises us, "Whatsoever ye shall ask in prayer, ye shall receive." Now I grant you that few people read the Bible these days, perhaps because they took Matthew too literally. But it doesn't matter, because today the good news of the Bible has been replaced by the Gospel according to Wellness. Pursuit of a good life has been replaced by the pursuit of the perfect life. "Everything ye pursue to become better, smarter, buffer, younger, more assertive, more caring, more inclusive, more diverse leads thee to a perfect life."

A few hundred years before Mathew suggested prayer as the vehicle to all things good, the Stoics proclaimed that virtue, the perfection of morality, leads to happiness and the good life. But virtue has to be more than a belief; it must thrive within us. Marcus Aurelius took this idea a few steps further by adding nobility of character and a steady temperament, modesty, and strength of character. All of these attributes require ownership. They do not waver in the storm of public opinion.

Today social media pictures an enviable life as a sequence of triumphs in which you overcome all the doubters and haters. But life is life, more peaks and valleys or yin and yang than ever-higher mountaintops which are surmounted employing a strong sense of self-esteem and the support of all your followers. This prescription is a recipe for disaster. Will Storr thinks that "People are suffering and dying under the torture of the fantasy self they are failing to become."

There was an old beer commercial that ran for a few years that claimed, "You only go around once in life, so you have to grab for all the gusto you can get." Salvation is out there in the bright lights, waiting for you to claim all that is rightfully yours because you, baby, are a rock star. But as the comic,

Louis CK, observed, why, if everything is awesome, everyone is miserable?

Svend Brinkmann notes that heaven as an external paradise has been replaced by attempting "to cram as much as possible into our relatively short time on the planet instead." Sounding very much like a modern-day Stoic, he argues that an ego-centered epicurean shopping spree will only lead to depression and loneliness. He admires integrity, self-control, loyalty, groundedness, obligation, and tradition. In the Jewish religion such a man is called a mensch,"a man of integrity and honor." And with this as a base, we stand firm. From a position of clarity and insight we do nothing. We don't bend. We don't attack, and we don't retreat. We do nothing, as Lao Tzu wrote, but we leave nothing undone.

Stand firm. Socrates taught and lived this truth. When he was charged by the authorities with corrupting the youth of Athens, out of deference to his exalted position he was offered banishment. He refused. Banishment would have been an admission of guilt. They sentenced him to death, and he drank the hemlock. He lived, taught, and died holding the truth tightly in his heart.

Years ago, a deranged war vet took issue with a Vietnamese Buddhist temple near his home. He entered the Dharma hall as the monks were meditating. One by one, he shot them in the head. When the police arrived, they saw that all the monks had remained seated with their eyes closed. They chose not to flee. They stayed immersed in the truth. True *mensches.*

81

One time I chose to simply live in a small guesthouse on Gnat Agi Pagoda Road in Bahan Township in Burma. I would forego all travel. Across from my guesthouse was a tea shop from which I could watch all of Burma, past and present, pass by. Further down the road was a stitcher lady who would alter and repair my longyis. And behind her was a monastery where I could meditate.

But the teahouse was my base. It had a mud floor. The roof and sidewalls were plastic sheeting stretched over bamboo poles lashed together. The stools and tables were children sized. Burmese pop blared all day. Perfect. Nothing to do and nowhere to go.

A father and his four-year-old son came by one morning. They both sat down and ordered a tea and a donut. After a moment or two the father was called home. He left his son at the teahouse. The four-year-old sat there and finished his tea and donut. He watched the passing scene. He bid good morning to friends as they walked by. After ten minutes or so the father returned. He ordered his son another tea. They both left soon thereafter. I watched them as they walked down the street hand in hand.

I read in the paper that Burma was rated as the poorest country in Asia. Somehow I don't think the boy knew this.

82

An old proverb says that "as a man thinketh, so he is." I'd like to alter this somewhat and proclaim that "as a man is conditioned, so he is." Oft-repeated behaviors, beliefs, views, and thought patterns define who we seem to be. This we feel is carved in stone, because we feel comfortable with what is familiar. And we surround ourselves with friends and family who reflect who we are. In a way this is very comforting, though it is a complete and fabricated myth.

Francis Crick, the co-discoverer of the DNA double helix who later delved into neuroscience, wrote that "You, your joys and sorrows, your memories and your ambitions, your sense of personal identity and free will, are in fact no more than the behavior of a vast assembly of nerve cells and their associated molecules." This is alien to the ideas of most people alive today. His description of who we are echoes the Buddha's discovery of insubstantiality over 2,500 years ago.

~ 83

Friendship. Where would we be without our friends? This is true for the homeless alcoholic who followed his friends' lead, quit school, took to the road, lived high and free until he lost his health, his integrity, and the courage to turn his life around. And this is true for most of the titans of Silicon Valley who succeeded thanks to friends. The founders of Google, Sergey Brin and Larry Page, have been friends since they were teenagers. Steve Jobs and the Woz were friends before they cofounded Apple. There is no doubt that our parents and friends play an important role conditioning and influencing, for better or worse, how we "choose" to live our lives.

We can't choose our parents, but we can choose our friends. The Buddha understood peer pressure, and so he strongly advised his monks to walk with like-minded people or walk alone. This is easier when one has a virtuous inner certitude which breeds a friendly independence from untoward influence. But even for the rest of us Jordan Peterson's Rule #3 states "Make friends with people who want the best for you."

Your teenage friends will influence your choices and hence shape the conditioning of your mind at a pivotal time in your mind's development. Be wary of peers who are discourteous and unkind to those outside their circle, who don't respect other opinions, who pull down others who aim to excel in an uncool undertaking, who lie, or who are cynical. Groupthink dictates that everyone in the group buy into the group dynamic. If you don't, you'll soon be on the outside looking in. Even though this is surely short-term gain for long-term pain, it remains difficult for any teenager to forego his support group.

Think of the attitudes and behaviors of your friends like the flu. Being close to them increases your chances of catching how they behave. The more you mimic their behaviors, the more comfortable you feel doing so. If they have a flu that gives you pause or makes you think twice, better to give them a wide birth. Remember, the more questionable their behavior, the more they want you with them. Misery, as my mother liked to say, likes company.

84

In her book, *Educated*, about growing up in a survivalist Mormon family where school was not an option and daily manual labor a necessity, Tara Westover relates how she found herself standing on a rooftop in England during a windstorm. Fellow students and a professor also on the roof hunched their shoulders and held on for dear life. Not Tara. She stood upright, hands in pockets. Her professor marveled at her lack of fear and asked her how she did it. "I've roofed my share of hay sheds," she explained. "I can stand in this wind, because I'm not trying to stand in it…The wind is just wind. You could withstand these gusts on the ground, so you can withstand them in the air. There is no difference. Except the difference you make in your head…If you could just control your panic, this wind would be nothing."

Conditions are just conditions, whether mental or meteorological.

85

In Maharashtra a few decades ago, my elderly meditation teacher was delivering his evening discourse when a deranged *sādhu* rushed at him from the back of the hall. The *sādhu* screamed incoherently and thrashed his arms about, ready to strike him. My teacher stopped his talk…and closed his eyes. He remained seated. The *sādhu* raised his arm to strike. He stopped his thrust midway, as if frozen. His arm fell limply to his side. He raised his arm again and threatened to strike only to freeze a second time. This continued until he dissolved in tears. He slumped back to his seat at the back of the hall. Guruji opened his eyes, smiled, and continued his talk.

Though happy with the outcome, I wasn't sure what had happened. My teacher had remained seated with eyes closed. He was a meditation master, so I knew he wasn't wishing the attack away in an out-of-sight, out-of-mind kind of way. And I was sure he was not oblivious to the harm that might have befallen him. He fully opened himself to the attack, almost welcoming it, free of fear. He didn't move, yet I knew he was locked in, alert to everything as it went down. Why did he do nothing? How could he just sit there and not react without some trepidation? And what stopped the attacker from striking? It was as if my teacher was in a protected cocoon, a force field that immobilized all attempts to harm him.

As strange as that sounded at the time, I realized many years later that he was indeed protected, as are we all when our intentions are pure, virtuous, unshakable, and full of loving-kindness.

86

Mettā is a Pāli word meaning loving-kindness. As the mind deconditions, many positive mind states arise. The emergence of these so-called divine abodes had been held back by the continually self-reinforcing habitual patterns that you thought defined you. As you allow these false images to be, without reinforcing them, they fade, allowing equanimity, compassion, sympathetic joy, and *mettā* to fill in the gaps. You can neither stimulate their arrival nor impede it. The divine abodes cannot be pressured. They arrive when they arrive.

Mettā should not be confused with romantic love. *Mettā* emanates from within. It spreads, more like mist than a jet spray. It is an indiscriminate healing force strong enough to convert serial killers from their evil ways. You don't have to take any action when this feeling arises, though action might ensue. "You" aren't taking action, because "you" may be conflicted as to what to do. *Mettā* is guided by insight as are the other divine abodes, so the action that is taken, when and if, will be the best possible for all concerned because the action is guided and even precipitated by wise understanding.

Wisdom arises when the unconscious biases that Tversky and Kahneman highlighted become conscious. We see our intentions behind our reasoning, and this insight into the preconditioned biases clarifies and gives pause to not only blind reactions, but also to what we previously deemed to be well-thought-out solutions. Even the act of donating millions for a new hospital complex loses its nobility if the intention is to elevate the status of the donor. Doing non-doing casts a light on our intentions. It balances our mind, tilting it towards honesty, and is ultimately liberating. The wealthy person, aware now that elevating his status was the primary motive for his donation, may still decide to go ahead with the gift. He just does so with greater understanding. Perhaps now the lettering of his name on his hospital wing will be in a smaller font...

Living the truth as it is revealed by doing non-doing aligns you with all the positive vibrations in the universe. You are a molecular collection, much the same as everything else. As you calmly abide and work in sync with the unconditioned mind, you are tuning in to the natural energy forces or vibrations in the universe. Similar to how a tuning fork works, your unconditioned mind tunes up with these universal energies to "protect" you. This is not some new age, speaking-with-angels shtick. Your unconditioned mind is actually now in tune with the laws of the universe. You are "protected" in fact by your own good deeds, your own loving-kindness, and your own unconditioned goodness.

This is a law of nature. Like jumping off a cliff to prove that gravity doesn't exist, acting in opposition to any law doesn't bode well. Divine retribution in its secular cloak of hubris awaits all who act out of greed, hatred, and delusion, all who act only to gratify their basic instincts, who ignore the basic awe, wonder, and grandeur of life's simple joys.

A balanced mind naturally attunes with the vibrations of all that is true and right, leading to a life lived with *sprezzatura.* This is an Italian word meaning graceful nonchalance, a perfect description of doing non-doing. You are graceful in all your actions, but it is a grace devoid of conditioning or practice. It comes not from an external desire to impress. It comes from within and without effort. *Sprezzatura* is wailing with grace.

If *sprezzatura* proves a bit of a stretch, just try to bear in mind that everyone you meet is fighting a great battle, and so cut them a bit of slack when they enter the express aisle at the local supermarket with thirteen items.

87

Two more salient points about *mettā*. *Mettā* must be tempered by wisdom. There is a parable from India of a kind man who came upon a frog in the middle of a busy road. Concerned that the frog might be crushed under the wheels of a bullock cart and feeling uncomfortable leaving him to his fate, he gently picked him up and transferred him safely to the side of the road from whence he had come. He took a step back to admire his handiwork, reveling in his generosity and kindness, when the snake who had chased the frog to the middle of the road, not believing his good fortune, quickly devoured the frog.

That parable was reflected here in Canada. We rescued a young child soldier from the Congo and deemed it our mission to save him from whatever retribution might await him in Africa. The immigration officials relocated him to Winnipeg, the gang capital of Canada. In less than a year he had been shot to death. Opening your heart should not entail closing your mind.

Mettā is inclusive but should not be equated with pity. Angulīmāla was a serial murderer in the days of the Buddha. His *nom du jour* came from his habit of cutting off the little fingers (*angulī*) of his victims and sewing them into a necklace (*mālā*). One day, looking for his next victim, he came upon the Buddha. The Buddha did not flee but suffused him in *mettā*. He treated him as a fellow human being suffering from greed, aversion, and delusion. He pointed out that Angulīmāla's misery was self-imposed, his wounds were self-inflicted, and his violence was unnecessary blind reaction.

Angulimala understood. In the end, the Buddha left him to take responsibility for his own life. He did so by becoming a monk. The Buddha did not offer him free tuition at a university. He offered him the opportunity to learn from his own mind. He did not offer him subsidized housing, he offered him homelessness. He did not offer him a lifelong pension, he offered him poverty. More was the problem; less was the answer. Action was the problem; doing nothing was the answer.

88

I volunteered with Mother Theresa at her Sisters of Charity palliative care hostel in Calcutta. My service was to help with the lunch meal as well as a certain undefined "nursing." The hostel was smaller than I had expected and the number of volunteers fewer than I had hoped. I thought a larger cohort would allow me a few days to get my bearings. That was not to be the case.

The clients were dying of every imaginable and communicable disease you could think of. Pneumonia. Aids. Tuberculosis. The most difficult for me were the lepers, because they looked like death more than the others who only sounded ill when they coughed or vomited up blood. I had only been there but a few minutes when a man fell out of bed and cracked his head. He bled profusely and couldn't get up. Immediately a Sister and a volunteer rushed to his aid. They cleaned him up, bandaged his head wound, and helped him back to bed. I was aghast at what I had just witnessed but not due to the outpouring of bodily fluids.

What troubled me most was that no one had used antiseptic plastic gloves in caring for the injured man, neither in dressing the wound nor in the later cleaning up. And this oversight was not a one-off. Bodily fluids were omnipresent, yet no one wore protection of any kind. At first glance the lack of protection seemed to me a recipe for disaster for the volunteers and the Sisters. I soon changed my mind.

As I continued to get a feel for the place, two things stood out. Firstly, the volunteers and especially the Sisters never stopped smiling. They exuded loving-kindness for even the most demanding patients, many of whom had a mental illness to go along with their physical problems. The more they were called on, the dirtier the job they were asked to do, the more their heart seemed to open.

Secondly, everyone serving appeared to be healthy, even radiantly so, and quite unperturbed about contracting any one of the myriad diseases present in that room which could end their lives. Touching a meal tray or just breathing had to bring you into contact with pathogens that we in the West fear so much. It was as if they had built-in immunity. I recalled my meditation master so many years before fending off the attack of the deranged *sādhu* by doing nothing. I realized he too seemed protected. Now I understood. He too appeared to be sheathed in a protective cocoon of loving-kindness.

As were all the volunteers at the hospice, the Sisters, and even a neophyte like me. *Mettā*. How else can you explain the lack of secondary infections in a third world hospice in Calcutta without a quarantine room and with only Dettol as a disinfectant when in the West we have strains of pneumococcal conditions and flesh-eating disease which exist only in hospitals? Our frontline workers wear hazmat suits when dealing with some of the same diseases the volunteers and the Sisters faced every day. And still they fall ill.

After the meal that first day of my service, we volunteers were given tea and a cookie. The tea was served in the same cups the patients used, and the cookies sat on the same plates. None of the eating utensils were ever sterilized, let alone saw soap. I happily accepted my thank you snack that day and every day after without trepidation. I never got so much as a sniffle.

89

I remember a *Sayadaw* (respected teacher) who lived in a remote monastery in upper Burma in the vicinity of Sagaing Hills. He was elderly and blind and very much loved. I visited him, excited to both meet a living legend and pay my respects. I was told to wait until he went for his evening walk when he would be with his attendant who could serve as a translator. There are few if any clocks at remote monasteries, so I had to wait until I saw a frail, very small monk holding onto the arm of another monk walking towards me. I recall being immersed in a quiet joy as he approached.

I was introduced to him, and he placed his hands on my face to see me better. He was giggling, bubbling with loving-kindness. I felt the strength of his *mettā*, which eliminated all the questions I had for him. I wanted to stay in that glow forever. I talked to him, though I don't remember what I said or what he replied. I just know that for ten minutes or so I basked in the glow of unconditional love.

As I also did every time I met Munindra, an *Anagārika* and teacher who lived for many years in Bodhgaya. Whenever I saw him, he greeted me with the same words, "It's so good to see you again." He would take both my hands in his, and he would smile. Years later I realized he must meet thousands of mendicants every year and probably says the same thing to every one else. He could not be expected to remember all the names or even the faces, but it didn't matter a jot. He exuded *mettā*, and there was no doubt that he would indeed be glad to see the person, any person, who so much as wanted to say hello to him.

Such unconditional love explains the enduring popularity of the Dalai Lama. He was once a guest at a resort in Mexico, where he was to be the primary speaker at a five-day conference. Every morning he would leave his bungalow and walk to the opulent conference center. As he stepped out of his room that first day, he saw the housemaid who was waiting to clean his room, standing off to the side of the path, with her eyes downcast. She had been trained to never engage any of the guests. Besides, she had no idea who this stooped old man in maroon robes was. She was a good Catholic and unversed in other religions and traditions. But this was the Dalia Lama, a man of infinite compassion and kindness for whom there are no Catholics, no Jews, and even no Buddhists. There were only human beings. He went to her. She looked at him. He smiled and said, "Good morning." And he continued his walk to the conference center.

The next morning as he opened his door, there was the cleaning lady waiting for him. Beside her were two of her fellow cleaning ladies. He came to all them and greeted them and went on his way. The next morning, he was greeted by the cleaning ladies and many others of the night workers, and by the last day of his stay almost every worker who could spare a few minutes of time stood along his path to be blessed by his smile. Most of them still had no idea who he was or even why they were there, except that they sure felt good when he walked by.

Mettā is a powerful force for good. It arises from doing non-doing. Ram Dass, the former Harvard psychology professor, LSD proponent, and guru attributed the ascendance of *mettā* and the other divine abodes to being nobody. The catch phrase of a recent documentary about his life entitled, "Becoming Nobody" proclaims, "Everyone's busy becoming somebody." They are wearing masks and clothing themselves in popular personas, suffocating their unconditioned emptiness from which loving-kindness emanates.

When you are nobody, devoid of any sense of I or mine, without attaching to a sense of I or mine, then all doing is non-doing. All is pure essence.

90

Most everyone is possessed by their possessions. I know people who are owned by their pets. I know others who build heated garages for their prized automobiles. My aunt bequeathed me an old rocking chair to which she added the caveat that I never change its mauve covering. In those years, I moved almost every year and carried that rocker to each apartment until its springs went and you couldn't sit in it without receiving a full rectal examination. And if you think about it almost everyone carries within themselves their own version of the mauve rocker, everything from political predilection and food idiosyncrasies to religious affiliation, odd habits, and proclivities, all resembling an old mauve rocking chair save for the wonky springs.

As I rid myself of many of my mental habitual possessions, an internal downsizing you might call it, I found myself de-cluttering my environs as well. For me this was a natural devolution. Never a fan of high tech, I devolved into Analogue Guy.

I now write in a notebook, usually a Moleskin that lies flat on the writing surface. I use a pen, not a Montblanc, but a relatively inexpensive Paper Mate InkJoy. I carry them in a leather roll-up pencil wrap from Korea with a cord closure. My backpack is so old it lacks a separate padded laptop compartment. I wear leather handmade shoes I purchased in 1980 and hiking boots, repaired once, of an even earlier vintage. Some might think this devolution came about from years of silent reflection in caves and mountaintops. Perhaps, but truth be told, I am of Scottish ancestry. My family and I are very frugal. I think my Zen-like austerity has more to do with Gaelic Presbyterian thriftiness than the sound of one hand clapping.

It does make sense that eventually your surroundings will reflect the insights that derive from your practice. However, these changes should be allowed to occur naturally. Don't force them upon yourself to convey an image of an enlightened being. I knew a guru with many followers who took a vow of silence, which he maintained for more than a decade. This is very laudable, provided it is motivated with noble intention. He carried a slate suspended by a string around his neck which he used to write short notes and observations for his devotees. I watched him carefully from afar as we both waited for our flight at the Delhi airport. He wrote a note every two minutes or so. His devotees would laugh or react in some other appropriate way. They never took their eyes off him. Between each epistle, it was obvious his mind was actively searching for the next witty or lucid observation. A vow of silence is a dog and pony show if inwardly the chatter continues unabated.

91

We needn't pause to figure out our next step in life. Life, real life, is there in the pause, in the quagmire of conflicting choices. We then choose one route and look for signs that this is the correct way to go. No doubt. "I have a good feeling about this" is more a sense of relief about finally choosing one route than a certainty that this route has been swept clean and is devoid of IEDs. Even the best choices cough up hairballs of unforeseen consequences.

This in no way means you can't choose to change direction, only that when the mind is beset with anger, craving, confusion, or jealousy any change you make is likely taken for the wrong (I hesitate to use the word) reason. In my thirties my life changed dramatically, but I did not orchestrate the change. One step revealed another small step that itself led naturally to another as old habits, anxieties, and desires fell to the wayside.

Mind matters most. If and when the mind is deconditioned, if and when one is a virtuous sort, keeping one's own counsel and not veering off the noble path, life unfolds naturally. This does not imply that all your dreams will be realized, your family will not suffer maladies, and there will be peace in the land. Steps have to be taken, interventions must be undertaken, voices at times need to be firm, especially when dealing with young children. Not to take steps is also a decision. Sometimes it is wise, other times it is a cop-out. However, doing non-doing keeps the extraneous voices at bay, alternatives and options remain on the table but are no longer screamed from the sidelines so that decisions are not so much taken but allowed to unfold. Tomorrow can only be clear when today is clear and it is being lived fully.

This from *Valdez is Coming* by Elmore Leonard: "They could be waiting or not waiting. Or he could have not seen the smoke. Or he could have continued with the woman southeast and been near the twin peaks by this evening. Or he never could have asked Diego Luz to help him. Or he never could have started this. Or he never could have been born. But he was here and he was pointing northwest instead of southeast because he had no choice." Just get on with it.

92

In the center of Igatpuri village is a street market. Vendors sit at stalls and sell their produce. Because every vendor sits in the same location, everyone knows what they sell. So all they need announce is the price. They don't try to out shout one another. They take turns. This creates a sort of chant, a back and forth. Except for the Hindi, it's a revival meeting in rural Alabama. At the main corner of the market are the banana sellers. First time there, I thought "do rupee" was the Hindi word for banana.

Towards the fringe of the market sit older women, widows perhaps, selling a few tomatoes or onions they have placed on a blanket. They sit there all day sheltered from the sun with an umbrella. They all carry a stick to thwack the dogs or cows who come by to grab a quick snack. They make very little money, but they get to sit with their friends all day and talk.

There is a new indoor market attached to the older one. The stalls are divided by concrete walls. You can't converse with your neighbor. The roof is tin. It is very hot in summer, and the roof holds the stench of rotting produce. The cows can't climb the stairs, so the vendors don't need sticks.

The villagers are proud of their new indoor market. It is a sign of progress, they say. The outdoor market is just for the tribals. They want me to shop at the indoor market. I tell them I have no caste just like the tribals. I think we should stick together. We tribals aren't so keen on progress.

93

According to Thoreau, "The mass of men lead lives of quiet desperation." I think when people read this, they focus on the word "quiet" as the problematic one in the sentence. Echoing Pascal, quiet isn't the problem, it is the inability to accept the quiet that leads to the desperation. We don't need to change our environs as much as change ourselves, because as Anaïs Nin wrote, "We see things not as they are, but as we are."

Just this year I went to meet some old friends for coffee. It was a warm and sunny day. I was early, so I walked along one of the main streets, one I had walked countless times. With no destination in mind I focused on my walking and my breath. I looked up the street, perhaps to get my bearings, though I was not looking for any particular markers or signposts. It was a warm and sunny day. As I looked, simply looked, the street scene was shimmering, as if I had been suddenly parachuted into a Renoir. It was mesmerizingly perfect. It was a miracle, and yet it was just what was really there to be seen. More to the point, this dappled shimmering essence is always there when the mind lets go of habitual patterns of perception.

It is only the thoughtful and the brave who consciously choose the small life. Some of those who choose the unfettered, free-roaming, grab-all-the-gusto-you-can life do so out of fear. They fear they might miss something. They will have no memories to ease their sunset years, they will have no stories with which to regale their friends. Their Facebook page will be devoid of likes, their Instagram account empty. What is the life without fame? What is the life without variety? What is life without goals and expectations?

Shimmering, perhaps?

94

With the death of a loved one, a grieving period is important, as is understanding how the mind works and how doing nothing with clear comprehension does not eliminate the grief. Once again, grieving is a natural condition of the mind. It is neither good nor bad. Some may be tempted to put on a happy face to demonstrate the powers of meditation. They can keep up the façade for a while. In time the effort to remain calm peters out. The suppressed grief returns in a myriad of ways later in life, when perhaps you cannot see a direct correlation between what you are presently dealing with and the death of someone close some months or even years before.

Allow the grief to come, give it lots of space and time. Don't force it, repress it, or indulge it. Let it be as it will, when it will, free of any judgment. You are the only one who really knows your relationship with the departed. It was probably complicated, as are most personal relationships. With their departure, feelings of guilt may arise. Again, this is natural. Take comfort in knowing that the departed loved one also felt some guilt and remorse over past uncivil words and deeds directed at you. Do not compound your grief, adding unneeded and unnecessary spices to the nuances of sorrow. Let it be until it isn't.

This will resemble more the proverbial two-steps-forward-one-step-back dance than a smooth gradual denouement. And for a few years some flashbacks of grief may arise, vestiges still remaining that stopped by to say goodbye before drifting into the ether.

When the grieving process has come to an end, don't feel that this is a slight to the deceased. You aren't forgetting them or letting them down. If they were close to you as a mentor and confidant, then they haven't really gone anywhere, for they and their way of being endure in your mind, in your attitudes, and in your very being. The best way now you can show your love is to get on with life.

95

Doing non-doing is a long path and is not always straightforward. To understand what you need to do and why and how is relatively easy, and in this regard I hope this little book has been a help. However, old habit patterns, especially latent tendencies, are pernicious. You may continue to be sidetracked by their beguiling beckoning to react. You may succumb from time to time. You may find the process hopeless. You may get frustrated. These reactions are also old habit patterns. It is as if you are at a masked ball, dancing with many different partners, all of whom keep exchanging their masks with each other. Still, do not give up. Have faith.

Faith is not blind belief. Faith is simple trust that those who walked the path of doing non-doing spoke the truth and more than that, lived that truth. From the Buddha and his contemporary Lao Tzu to the Stoics of Greece and Rome right up to present-day masters such as S.N. Goenka, Ajahn Sumedho, and the Dalai Lama, the teachings reflect the experiential insights of thousands of enlightened beings. The truth and guidance they bequeath us came not from God or from some other mystical being who descended from the heavens. The truth came from their own investigation, their own experience, as it will for you from your own self-discovery. However, when wrestling with the futility of existential angst, faith in both the teaching and the teachers will see you through.

Sometimes very fearful mind states arise. These can be difficult to deal with. How do you do non-doing when you are full of fear? In cases like this it is best to bring into the mind its opposite trait: make a joke of it for example. At times like this I remember an old black and white "horror" movie that came out in 1944 starring the great Charles Laughton. It was entitled "The Canterville Ghost," based on a short story of Oscar Wilde's. The ghost in question haunted his old castle and made it uninhabitable. A platoon of American GIs was billeted there before their departure for the front. They were all young men and very tired after a long sea voyage. In no time the men were fast asleep on their cots. The ghost didn't want the men mucking up his castle, so at midnight he came out and did his haunting bit with chains and moaning and blood-curdling screams. The GIs would have none of it. They laughed at the whole thing and made fun of the ghost. They threw their boots at him and parodied his act. The ghost had never been treated in such a manner. Everyone he scared before raised their hands and ran away. The ghost slinked away to the catcalls of the young and brash soldiers.

This is the attitude to take whenever difficult mind states like fear, doubt, and worry arise. Laugh at them and welcome them. The mind is big enough to find a space for them. Just tell them to be quiet and to go about their business but be sure to clean up after themselves when they go. Along with a half-smile, sitting with strong determination to remain still without fidgeting, shaking, and getting up, not moving at all allows your body to emulate a serene boreal lake. This sets a stable physical base, enabling your perplexed, reactive mind as much time as it needs to follow suit.

A friend had a bumper sticker on his VW bus that read, "I feel better now that I've given up hope." The flip side of the hope coin is fear. When you say you hope for success or even enlightenment, you are also implying that you fear failure or remaining in delusion. The further implication is that you have to acquire something spiritual or transcendent. But doing non-doing is not Amazon.com. You are not on a shopping spree. You are calmly abiding hopes and fears and all the mind states that have been self-perpetuated and reinforced on a daily basis. Let them be.

96

My teacher in India eventually attracted so many students that he began to appoint assistants to lead retreats on their own. I began assisting him in 1996 and soon was made a senior assistant teacher. I led ten-day retreats throughout Canada, the United States, England, Myanmar, and India. I especially enjoyed addressing the many issues my students faced, most of whom were dealing with the daily shock of seeing into the skittishness of their minds for the first time. I was on a mission to spread the teachings, I had status and prestige within the community of meditators, and my personal practice was strong. How my life had changed!

A teacher conducting a retreat spends most of the time alone. Your meals show up at your door, you go for long walks by yourself, and your only company might be an old newspaper if you are lucky. When the retreat was over, I hustled down to the kitchen area where I had breakfast with the staff serving on the retreat. I drank gallons of tea, ate close to a whole loaf's worth of toast, and talked up a storm. I dismissed this fondness for socializing as nothing more than an old habit pattern that inevitably would fall away.

It didn't. And slowly I realized I had bought into an idealization of the world-travelling Dhamma teacher, a lone reed, living on the charity of others, spreading the good news. I liked being seen that way. It was how I viewed monks and recluses since I was a child. I idolized those with a mission who shunned society. I liked being seen that way. I viewed any attachment I still had to social interactions as an encumbrance that would soon fall away. Meanwhile, I believed my imagined and idealized self to be real.

Doing non-doing was and is my life. But I had turned it into a lifestyle, a public display of my commitment. It didn't hurt that my supposed asceticism took me to India every year, where I mucked about with my mates from all over the world and drank enough chai and ate enough samosas to warrant a yearly ECG. I wore longyis and khadis I bought from the Gandhi Bhavan and wove Hindi and Burmese into my stories, allowing only the cognoscenti of the Asian Dhamma circuit to understand.

The teachings of the Buddha are paramount, and the insights that arise are profound. But it matters not a jot what color your robe is. I realized that for many of the years that I trekked about South Asia I had kept my posh apartment in a luxury high-rise on the Rideau River in Ottawa. And I had never quit my day job as a schoolteacher with its pension and dental plans. Slowly it dawned on me that my robe was always colored in more mundane hues than the monastics I wanted to emulate. I hadn't been living a lie exactly, but I had been living a hope. I had hoped that my renunciant ideal would eventually fit me. I hoped I would grow into that person. It was not to be.

It was about this time that I met a young woman from Korea doing graduate work in Vermont. For the summer she had arranged to help a good friend of mine with her newborn third son to familiarize herself with the ways of the West before she started school. As I write this, today is our twentieth wedding anniversary. We have two teenage sons, a bungalow, and I drive an SUV.

Nothing that really matters has changed. Stuff happens and I deal with it. This was the practice of the Buddha. The stuff that comes up is different than when I was a "Dharma Bum." There is an old saying that when you buy a goat, you get goat problems. Even celibate world-traveling vegetarian Dhamma teachers have problems. Doing non-doing applies to all: princes, paupers, and mendicants alike.

Everything changes. I learned, though, that even things that changed may change again.

97

How long will it take to be enlightened? This is such a first-world question. We want the truth and we want it now, to paraphrase Jim Morrison. There is no answer to that question, because it is the wrong question. And what's more, enlightenment is not simply an answer, similar to the woman in Saks Fifth Avenue who asked how much the fur coat cost in the window who was told, "Madam, if you have to ask, you can't afford it." Nevertheless, let's respond with the truth rather than attempting an answer to the wrong question.

Our problems really begin when we blindly and conditionally react to negative or euphoric or deluded mind states. Our task is to do nothing, calmly abiding whatever arises in the body/mind. We are not eliminating their existence like some kind of drone missile but enveloping these conditions with awareness and equanimity, rendering them impotent and nonoperative. They have been neutralized to the unadorned status of a thought, a blip in the cosmic consciousness. This blip, this thought is now unconditioned or maybe better, deconditioned, and we are just seeing into the workings of the mind, moment by moment, free of contamination.

For that moment of seeing, just seeing, you are a Buddha. You are enlightened. "How long did that take?" is an unnecessary question because there you are at this moment. You now know that enlightenment is within your grasp, like Tiger winning the Masters. The day after his victory he returned to the course and hours of practice. And so do you. If the next moment is full of strong emotion and you get carried away, at a certain level of consciousness, you know this is conditioning, this is not me, this is blind reaction, and you bring yourself back to awareness. This is the practice, and over time, the time you spend aware with clear understanding increases, and you come to better understand the Zen maxim that there is no beginning to enlightenment, no ending of practice.

What you have achieved is a kind of freedom. Seeing the mind as it is for the first time loosens the Gordian knot of servitude just enough to chip away at any doubts you may have, any fears that might arise, any craving that continues to rock you, and any hatred that carries you away. A sculptor too chips away the extraneous rock from a block and reveals the statue hidden inside. You as well chip away at the detritus of conditioning moment by moment, revealing an unconditioned you. Everything has changed, but nothing is different. Or everything is different, but nothing has changed.

A good friend spent years in India meditating on the same hilltop as I did. He returned home and for a while lived back with his parents. Someone asked his mother if she noticed a difference in her son after years of doing non-doing. She paused and replied, "Well, I think he's put on a little weight."

98

There is an old story about a young seeker who asks the abbot of a nearby monastery for guidance on how to become enlightened. The abbot declines his request but sends him to a shoemaker in a nearby village. The abbot assures him that the shoemaker will help him achieve enlightenment. The young seeker went to find the shoemaker, with one caveat from the abbot: "Learn everything you can from the shoemaker, but don't ask him anything spiritual."

The shoemaker welcomed the young man and took him on as his apprentice. Over the ensuing years, the master shoemaker taught his young apprentice how to make shoes and how to repair them. Shoes came into the shop and shoes left the shop. The two of them worked side by side. They would break for tea and for an evening meal. At the end of the day, they would sit outside on a bench and watch the stars come out. Their communication consisted of few words. Nothing important was left unsaid.

It was a peaceful and easy life for the seeker. It was easy for him to refrain from asking the shoemaker anything spiritual, for he seemed to have very few questions. His mind was still and shimmered with *mettā*. In time the old shoemaker passed on. The seeker remained in the shop. He knew the trade well and was now a master. Shoes continued to come in and leave the shop.

In time the abbot paid him a visit. He said, "You have learned your trade well. You are at peace. One day I may send you a young seeker. Please teach him all you know about shoe making. Do not teach him anything spiritual." And with that the abbot returned to the monastery.

In the same vein, I hope you have learned something from this little book. And that you are ready to take your first steps or more steps to a life of peace and insight. Like the shoemaker, I too have not spoken to you of anything spiritual. When seeing, just see. Do nothing else. Nothing. Don't even *try* to do non-doing, but let it be done.

Charles Schulz, the creator of Peanuts, once said, "My life has no purpose, no direction, no aim, no meaning, and yet I'm happy. I can't figure it out. What am I doing right?" I don't know what he is doing right either, but I can almost guarantee you that Mr. Schulz was not looking for happiness. Looking for it assumes it is out there somewhere. It isn't out there. It isn't even somewhere. Even doing non-doing, calmly abiding the ebb and flow of the unconditioned mind will not lead to happiness, but in time happiness will find you. It knows where you live, and though you may come and go, happiness knows you never leave home.

And just before you put the book down, a final story…

The aging abbot, now nearly blind, assembled forty of his most senior monks.

"Tomorrow we will visit the Cave of the Sacred Emerald Buddha. The path is long, the climb hard, but the destination is well worth the effort. Rest well tonight. We leave at dawn."

The abbot was right about the path and the climb. The monks were glad they had brought plenty of water with them. They marveled at the endurance of the abbot, who was far ahead of the slower monks. They also wondered how the abbot knew the route so well, for he had seldom ventured beyond the monastery boundaries except for *pindipat.*

Just before nightfall, exhausted and bedraggled, the assembly arrived at a small fissure in the rock face. There they rested for a few minutes before the abbot addressed them.

"This is the entrance to the Cave of the Sacred Emerald Buddha. You may enter one at a time. Find a place inside facing the statue and let us meditate until first light. Out of respect for the Triple Gem, let us do so in silence."

The monks did as they were told, entering with a quiet reverence tinged with anticipation. Though the first to enter had lit a few candles, it still took a while for their eyes to adjust to their new surroundings. A few began to meditate immediately, but most scanned the cave, looking for the Sacred Emerald Buddha.

However, the cave was bare—no statue, no emeralds, nothing that remotely could be described as sacred, except for a pile of stones that appeared to be the focus of the abbot's attention. Out of respect for him and the guidance he had provided over the past decades, the monks bowed before the pile of stones, closed their eyes, and meditated.

At first light, the abbot spoke. "For many of you, this visit to the Cave of the Sacred Emerald Buddha may be your last. It is believed that the Sacred Buddha is offering some of its power to you in the form of the many emeralds that have come loose. These emeralds are given freely. You may come forward and take one emerald each away with you for a while. It will inspire your meditation practice."

Most of the monks were too exhausted from the climb and the nightlong meditation session to question the abbot's request. A few speculated that his ailing eyesight had led him to the wrong cave. But whether from tiredness, confusion, or simple respect for their aging abbot, the monks came forward one at a time to select a stone from the pile of rubble. The abbot watched each monk in turn, paid his respects, and was the last to leave the cave.

Two weeks later the abbot again assembled the forty senior monks. "A while ago, you visited the Cave of the Sacred Emerald Buddha. Each of you took away with you one of the loosened emeralds from the statue. I hope it has inspired you to practice diligently. I ask that by noon today you return your emerald to me."

A few monks repressed a smile. Others avoided eye contact with their friends out of fear that they might laugh and unduly embarrass their aging abbot. They all, however, returned to their khutis and retrieved what they had removed from the pile of rubble in the cave.

The abbot waited in the main courtyard, unperturbed by the blazing sun overhead. He carried an old begging bowl. As each monk arrived with his "precious" stone, the abbot slid the top off the bowl. He was sure even he could see the glint of the sun as it reflected off the deposited emeralds.

One by one the monks deposited their stones. And with each, the abbot removed the lid and waited for the sun's reflection to startle his failing eyes. He waited almost the entire morning. No stone returned the sun's rays. No emeralds glistened in the begging bowl. Thirty-nine senior monks had come and gone. Only Sumangala, the kitchen manager, who helped to organize the once-a-day meal, had yet to arrive. He had been busy all morning in the monastery kitchen. But he was also known to meditate in the densely forested far reaches of the monastic grounds to avoid the afternoon study period. Some monks thought him to be illiterate, but none questioned his meditation strengths.

When he finally arrived just before noon, he smiled at the aging abbot. The abbot removed the lid from the begging bowl. Sumangala unfurled the lower hem of his robe, removed his stone, and dropped it into the bowl. A ray of reflected sunlight arose from the bowl. At this, it was the abbot who smiled.

"My eyesight is not very good. Tell me, Sumangala, what do you see in the bowl?"

"Why, emeralds, of course."

"And so there are, Sumangala. What did you see in the cave?"

"Just as you described it, Ajahn. An emerald Buddha statue on a mantle comprised of rubies and diamonds. It was magnificent. Oh, that your eyesight was better."

"Sumangala, you are right. My eyesight is failing. My hearing could be better. I no longer need to shave my head! My time as abbot has come to an end. I am asking you to be the next abbot. Now, return these emeralds to the Cave of the Sacred Emerald Buddha. Mark well the path you take today, for you will not return there for many years. When it is time for you to appoint a new abbot, assemble your most senior monks and lead them to the cave. Meditate there for the evening. Ask each monk to take with them one of the loosened emeralds. Two weeks later, collect the emeralds. Most will deposit only worthless rubble. Only one will bring you an emerald. Only one will truly have seen the Sacred Emerald Buddha. Only one will display the insight to see perfection in a dark and empty cave. And only one will carry that perfection away with him. He will be your successor, as you will be mine."

"Ajahn, how will I find the Cave of the Sacred Buddha?"

"If you see emeralds where others see worthless pebbles and if you see Buddha relics where others see piles of rubble, you already know the right path." And with that the abbot returned to his khuti, and Sumangala set off once again for the Cave of the Sacred Emerald Buddha.

May you too see emeralds when others see rubble. May you too see miracles in the mundane. May you uncover your true Buddha nature, which you have never lost.

Acknowledgements

This book is a compilation of teachings, so I would be remiss to not share any merits I have gained with my teachers.

Roshi Albert Low and his wife, Jean, remain an inspiration for me. Roshi embodied strength and compassion, displaying little distinction between how he lived his life and how the Buddha expected his disciples to comport themselves. The bar he set was extremely high, and if I have come close to touching that standard it is only because I stood on his shoulders.

I was fortunate to be with Āchariya S.N.Goenka in India in the earlier days at Dhammagiri. His humor, his clarity, and his *mettā* inspired me to pick myself up time after time and simply "start again."

I was preparing to take robes under Bhante Gunaratana at his forest monastery in West Virginia. He was a much beloved monk and for good reason. He was an author of many Dhamma books and had a twinkle in his eye. His books were good, but oh, his twinkle! When you are with him, he is without pretense despite his standing as the pre-eminent Theravada monk in the West. Though the robes were never taken, he guided me to understand that practice is a lifetime commitment.

I met Ajahn Viradhammo when he first returned to Canada after many decades at Wat Pah Nanachat in Thailand. He was meant to be in robes. I bumped into him one afternoon at our local public library and thanks to his lack of ego, it was the most natural thing in the world to be talking with a shaven-headed monastic in ochre robes on a cold winter's day. He embodies the teaching.

Dr. Nalini Devdas has been a friend, mentor, and teacher of mine for over forty years, and they threw away the mold when she retired for dedication to her field of study, to all her students, and to hard work. However close I came to that degree of effort was because of her.

This book would still be wishful thinking if it weren't for the kind and generous guidance of Bill Hart, once a teacher of mine and now a dear friend and mentor who read over my rough draft and gently suggested improvements. He has also done the same thing whenever he found me wavering. I am forever in his debt.

ABOUT PARIYATTI

Pariyatti is dedicated to providing affordable access to authentic teachings of the Buddha about the Dhamma theory (*pariyatti*) and practice (*paṭipatti*) of Vipassana meditation. A 501(c)(3) nonprofit charitable organization since 2002, Pariyatti is sustained by contributions from individuals who appreciate and want to share the incalculable value of the Dhamma teachings. We invite you to visit www.pariyatti.org to learn about our programs, services, and ways to support publishing and other undertakings.

Pariyatti Publishing Imprints

Vipassana Research Publications (focus on Vipassana as taught by S.N. Goenka in the tradition of Sayagyi U Ba Khin)

BPS Pariyatti Editions (selected titles from the Buddhist Publication Society, copublished by Pariyatti in the Americas)

Pariyatti Digital Editions (audio and video titles, including discourses)

Pariyatti Press (classic titles returned to print and inspirational writing by contemporary authors)

Pariyatti enriches the world by

- disseminating the words of the Buddha,
- providing sustenance for the seeker's journey,
- illuminating the meditator's path.

www.ingramcontent.com/pod-product-compliance
Lightning Source LLC
LaVergne TN
LVHW090945080826
845145LV00003B/893

* 9 7 8 1 6 8 1 7 2 3 8 1 5 *